HOW TO BE A
Billion Dollar Persuader

HOW TO BE A
Billion Dollar Dollar Persuader

MATTHEW J. CULLIGAN

ST. MARTIN'S PRESS
NEW YORK

Other books by Matthew J. Culligan:
THE CURTIS-CULLIGAN STORY
HORRID HOROSCOPES
HOW TO KILL STRESS BEFORE IT KILLS YOU
THE QUEST FOR THE GALLOPING HOGAN

Copyright © 1979 by Matthew J. Culligan
All rights reserved. For information, write:
St. Martin's Press, Inc., 175 Fifth Avenue, New York, N.Y. 10010.
Manufactured in the United States of America
Library of Congress Catalog Card Number:79-16391

Library of Congress Cataloging in Publication Data

Culligan, Matthew J.   1918-
  How to be a billion dollar persuader.

  1. Selling. 2. Persuasion (Psychology)
I. Title.
HF5438.25.C84   658.85   79-16391
ISBN 0-312-39588-4

Dedication

To Moses, Jesus Christ, Buddha, Mohammed, Martin Luther, Thomas Jefferson, Abraham Lincoln, Franklin Delano Roosevelt, John F. Kennedy, Robert Francis Kennedy, Winston Churchill, Mahatma Gandhi, Kemel Attatürk, Charles de Gaulle, Chairman Mao, David ben-Gurion, Patrick Pearse and the Irish leaders of the "Glorious Folly" of the Easter '16 uprising, Anwar Sadat, John Milton, George Bernard Shaw, Rachel Carson, Alex Haley (author of *Roots*), Henry Ford, Jean Monnet, St. Francis of Assisi, Albert Schweitzer, Sigmund Freud, Carl Jung, Arnold Toynbee, Martin Luther King, Jr., Margaret Mead, and all the other great persuaders who changed their nations and the world.

And to Pope John Paul II, Gerald Green (author of *Holocaust*), the founders of the Anglican-Catholic Church, Daniel Patrick Moynihan, Teddy Kennedy (who could if he would), and the other potential persuaders who could make the difference in the future.

Contents

Prologue
★★★★★★★★★★★★★★★★★★★★★★★★★★★★

You can be a Billion Dollar Persuader.

And just what is that? It is the developed skill of getting exactly what you want in life when you want it. It is living the kind of life you want to live and being in control of your career, your personal relationships, and your future. The art of persuasion, used morally and intelligently, really can get you just about anything you want. A detailed explanation of why and how this is possible, based on actual experience, is what this book is all about.

The most obvious examples of successful persuasion are found in sales, and so a great many of the lessons in this volume will relate to persuasion as it is practiced in selling products and services. But the lessons here are just as relevant to virtually every human interaction in which one individual attempts to alter another's actions or decisions to conform to his own.

For example, in getting a raise or a promotion, an employee must, through his words and actions, persuade his boss to decide in his favor. In an election—from president of the PTA to president of the United States—the candidate must persuade voters that he is the best person for the job and that they should cast their votes for him. A writer, scientist, community worker, or legislator is often in the position of persuading others (a publisher, a foundation, a government agency, fellow legislators) that a certain project should be accepted, supported, authorized, and/or funded.

Persuading, as opposed to forcing our will on others—often with the use or threat of violence—is a uniquely human activity. Animals, through real or ritual combat, attain dominance in their habitat or acquire the necessities of survival. Regrettably, human beings do the same, but we also have the option of attaining our goals through the peaceful arts of persuasion.

I would imagine that the arts of persuasion—argument, debate, demonstration, compromise, etc—were first practiced soon after our species discovered (or invented) language, the *sine qua non* of persuasion. I can well imagine neighboring troglodytes bickering over the relative values of a stone axe and the fruits of a day's hunting until one convinces that other that the axe is worth two rabbits and an antelope, and the trade is made. By the time our ancestors developed agriculture, the growth of commerce, specialization, and the complexity of life had produced money (as a measure of value) and full-time persuaders in the persons of sales agents, brokers, negotiators, and arbitrators. The further advance of civilization produced, in turn, over the millennia, lawyers, rhetoricians, polemicists and propagandists, advertising copywriters, public relations experts, marketing and sales engineers, and motivational psychologists.

Throughout history, the most effective of these persuaders have done both great good and great evil. The good ones, the ones who were constructive, have convinced the rest of us to accept a new, more advanced, more ethical way of life (Moses, Jesus, Buddha), to forsake violence (Gandhi), to pursue a radically new form of government (Hamilton, Madison, and Jay in *The Federalist Papers*), to cooperate instead of warring with each other (Jean Monnet, founder of the European Common Market), and so on. The evil ones, the ones bent on purely personal gain or driven by fear, have, at the cost of misery, death, and destruction, persuaded us to make war on our neighbors, to hate and revile those who are different from us, and to deny our own humanity.

Most persuasion, however, is neutral, in that it is a gain for the persuader and a gain (or at least not a loss) for the one who was persuaded. After all, if a copywriter succeeded in getting you to buy this book through the jacket copy or an advertisement, a fair exchange has taken place; you have been persuaded to spend a small part of your disposable income for this volume and now have the book, and the publisher, bookseller, and author have your money to divide among them. (Quite naturally, I am assuming that this book is worth having and that you will gain more than the physical book when you buy it.) If you convince your boss to give you a raise (again we'll assume you deserve it), you gain extra income and the boss will have a happier, more loyal, more productive employee.

The elements of persuasion, the tools and techniques used, and the attitudes and skills of the successful persuader are the subject of this volume. In these pages I will not only explore all the facets of persuasion in detail, but I will also show that, in each kind of persuasion, the tools and techniques, the skills and attitudes, and the steps to be followed are the same; the apparent differences are simply ones of degree.

Very briefly, the steps in successfully persuading someone—changing him, influencing his actions, getting a favorable decision—are as follows:

>Clear identification of your objective
>Research
>Planning the presentation
>Making contact
>Delivering the message
>Follow-through, if necessary

In addition, the successful persuader must have or develop the following:

Belief in the value or importance of the product, service, or
  objective/goal
Commitment to succeeding; zeal
Self-confidence; ego
Empathy (the ability to see a situation from another's point of
  view)
Communication skills, both active and passive
Imagination
Patience
Discipline
Competitiveness.

These are the elements of persuasion that will be treated in this
book. First, however, I should introduce myself and establish
my qualifications for telling you what persuasion is all about.

I have been a persuader all of my life, and in a thirty-year
business career I literally sold a billion dollars worth of products
and services. As a boy, I was a ringleader among my comrades
and excelled in persuading them to go along with my
schemes—and in persuading any number of authority figures,
including parents, teachers, shopkeepers, and the local cop, to
let us go when my plans went awry. In school I was known as a
"skin of the teeth" student. If the passing grade was 65, I would
get 66. If the grade D was failing, I would bring home C-minus.
The exception was English in which I was always an A student,
followed by geography, almost always B-plus. I qualified for the
debating team and starred in the seniors' school play.

In the United States Army I earned a commission, and except
for one dumb move (volunteering for the infantry), I escaped
onerous duty and boredom by writing articles and getting cozy
with the colonel's daughter.

My business career was described at various times thusly: the
Boy Wonder; Supersalesman; Miracle Man; Troubleshooter
Extraordinary; and one of the three best marketing executives in
America. I had some detractors, but somehow, by some design,
successful persuasion, and much luck, I was an advertising
manager at thirty, an executive vice president of the NBC

Television Network and president of the NBC Radio Network at thirty-seven, a top corporate executive of McCann Erickson-Interpublic at forty, and chairman of the board and president of the Curtis Publishing Company at forty-two. During those years as a businessman I raised hundreds of millions of dollars for the Boy Scouts, the United Jewish Appeal, the United Way, and other public service organizations. At the peak of my business career I was the target for a combined libel and slander attack in which I learned about the destructive aspects of persuasion.

That experience was a crossroads for me. One road led to bitterness and recrimination and self-pity. The other to careful review and introspection. Why had it happened? To what degree was I responsible for its happening?

One dear friend performed a service for which I was perpetually grateful. He was a Billion Dollar Persuader in his own right, but far more of a management scientist than I. John Lawrence Burns, after a good career in the management of manufacturing plants and general managements, became the managing partner of Booz, Allen and Hamilton, the largest management consulting company in America. In that capacity he worked on very intimate terms with General David Sarnoff, the builder of the Radio Corporation of America (RCA). At one point, General Sarnoff thought he was losing control of the gigantic company, which was largely run by self-made men like himself. He brought John Burns in as president and supported his reorganization of RCA. We became friends and golfing partners despite the difference in our positions and relative ages. At the peak of the controversy, when I felt very confident that I had won the battle against my opponants, John Burns invited me to his office for a preluncheon chat. That very morning I had convinced the Executive Committee to fire the ringleaders of a group that was attempting to take over the company. He looked at me with compassion as I told him of that victory. He said, "Joe, you must get yourself psychologically prepared for the first major defeat of your life. There has been too much publicity, too many rumors, the Board of Directors will have to make you the fall guy. But, my friend, always remember this. Success is wonderful, but it doesn't teach you very much." I showed some amazement at that statement. He went on, "It's true. A long, continuous success simply confims a man's very good opinion of himself. A defeat makes a man reevaluate himself. You will come out of this a much better man and manager." So, I turned my back on bitterness and recrimination and spent considerable time in self-evaluation. I truly believe that first, major defeat did what John Burns anticipated; I was a better man and better manager because of it.

HOW TO BE A
Billion Dollar Persuader

1

Where it All Began

★★★★★★★★★★★★★★★★★★★★★★★★★★★★

There probably wasn't much persuasion in the world before man became an agricultural and social being around twelve thousand years ago in ancient Mesopotamia. Prior to that time, man, pitifully weak in size and natural armament in a hostile world, was a marauding, hunting animal. It is now generally accepted that man survived and evolved partly because of his unique ability to choose between fight and flight, and his development and use of tools and weapons. The astounding discoveries of the Leakey family in Olduvai Gorge in Tanzania, enriched the human race in identifying the approximate location of the beginning of agricultural man.

The human beings who did opt for the life of farming and domesticating animals were forced to learn to live with one another on more and more complicated levels. Disputes could not be settled by breaking heads or throwing spears, so the social order began to take form. Meditate with me for a moment and see if we can visualize how it might have happened.

When the Nile seasonally overflowed, the people who raised their crops in the rich earth along the banks were forced to retreat to higher ground on both sides and await the return of the river to its normal level. It can well be imagined how they would argue and perhaps fight over the land they believed was theirs before the waters rose. Then one day one inspired man noted that by sighting along unmovable objects on both ridges it was possible to locate, with some accuracy, the farmlands below. That rock, to that tree, to that stump was the beginning of triangulation, which became the beginnings of geometry. The genius who made that discovery was almost certainly destined to become a leader, and it would follow that he would be the custodian of the records that were probably drawn on the walls of caves. Since he had these duties, he probably could not spend his time farming. Because he was providing an essential service to the rest of the farmers, they probably did not object to supporting him in some fashion. The obvious method would be by giving him a part of their crops, then perhaps, some clothes and ornaments. In those first permanent societies it is likely that people continued to "wear their wealth" as their nomadic forebears had done.

Sooner or later, it would seem to me, it became necessary to protect the allocations of the farmland, so our leader selected what in effect became the world's first police force, and thus began taxation, since these guards could not maintain their own farms while doing their duty.

The key fact of this marvelous human drama was the change of these human beings from savage, nomadic hunters and gatherers, to relatively peaceful, agricultural beings who had burgeoning scientific, political, and administrative systems as adaptive realities. Concomitant with change was, of course, growing interpersonal relationships, communication, and persuasion. Despite the miraculous changes occuring during these thousands of years, mankind did not lose his flight or fight response. When a human being is threatened today, or thinks he is being threatened, his autonomic nervous system causes the same kind of physiological responses experienced by our ancestors. The heart beats more rapidly. Chemical substances, produced by glands and poured into the blood stream, prepare the body for fighting or fleeing. There are two systems at work in this flight or fight response. One is known as the *exteroceptive* system: our senses of sight, smell, hearing, touch, and taste. The other is known as the *interoceptive* system. This causes the heart to beat faster, the blood to concentrate in the brain and the major muscles of the body, and the body's cooling system to accelerate (increased perspiration). I will bring this from the theoretical to the practical with this simple illustration.

You are sitting, relaxed, in your living room, breathing normally; your hands are warm and dry; your eyelids are blinking about once every three seconds in the natural process of lubricating and cleaning your eyes. You have a sense of safety and well-being without particularly thinking about it.

Suddenly you smell smoke. You are aroused by the natural fear of fire instilled in your psyche eons ago in your human and animal ancestors. Then you hear the siren of an approaching fire engine. You leap to the window and see the blinking lights of the fire engine approaching your building. Your heart rate has increased, your hands have become colder, your palms moist, and your breathing has become rapid and shallow. Your blinking rate has increased to a steady flutter. Your flight or fight mechanism is now primed.

But then the fire engine goes on by; you go to the door of your apartment, open it, and notice the faint smell of your apartment's incinerator. You realize that it has been a false alarm, but your heart is still beating rapidly, your hands are cold and clammy, and your sense of security and well-being has been shattered, and will not return for some time. The chemicals poured into your bloodstream by your interoceptive system will lose their potency in time, and you will return to normal.

There are countless such episodes in everyday life, but the fortunate among us get conditioned to many of them. The point I am making is about the involuntary self-deception that goes on in all our lives. Our senses can deceive us. Immediately before writing this chapter I was exposed to the dreadful facts and speculations about the mass suicide and murder in Guyana of the over nine hundred members of the People's Temple. The poison they took voluntarily or were forced to take was cyanide. I know, from a variety of detective stories, that cyanide has the odor of almonds. I could not bring myself to order one of my favorite dishes, filet of sole amandine, because of the involuntary revulsion to almonds. That was involuntary self-deception leading to a conscious decision against an innocent dish.

I make this point in the very first chapter of this book to highlight the most important challange to the Billion Dollar Persuader. The most important single bit of persuading you can do is to persuade yourself that your goals in life are known and comprehended to the greatest degree possible, and that you understand the dangers of self-deception and learn how to overcome what I believe should be listed as the Eighth Deadly Sin.

2

How the Billion Dollar Persuader Overcomes Self-deception

★★★★★★★★★★★★★★★★★★★★★★★★★★★

The absolute first essential the Billion Dollar Persuader should know is to what degree self-deception stands in the way of the Greek ideal of beauty and diversity. Socrates admonished one to "know thyself." When he made that recommendation, knowing oneself was largely a matter of memory; what family, friends, and enemies told us about ourselves by their words and actions, and the subconscious sense of whatever we seemed to be destined for. In our time we are very fortunate in having new techniques and technologies for clear observation of ourselves—physically, mentally, and spiritually. These can reverse self-deception. How can each of us work toward this goal? Fortunately, there are many specific programs available, but they demand time and money. An alternative is extensive reading of the competant materials that have been and are being produced.

I was most fortunate in getting involved quite early in what is known as self-regulation training. Biofeedback became a promoter's name for self-regulation training—to its disadvantage. I was impelled toward self-regulation training by the greatest single shock of my adult life: a bleeding ulcer that brought me within a half-hour of cardiac arrest from loss of blood. The self-deception was understandable. I appeared to be a completely healthy man, passing life insurance examinations for policies worth $5 million insisted upon by a group of banks who had loaned $38 million to the company I was hired to save from bankruptcy. Certain laboratory tests would have disclosed that changes in my life style brought about by the business crisis were causing physical changes. One of these changes was an increase in the level of hydrochloric acid in my digestive system. When this increase was coincident with overwork, plus heavy smoking and drinking, the acid ate into a vein in my duodenum and caused internal bleeding. And this was despite my feeling well and looking healthy! That is an example of physical self-deception.

During the same period I was deceiving myself about the state of my marriage and my relationship with my children. I was providing a beautiful home, education, recreation, clothes, and cars for my wife and my four children. I deceived myself that all was well. Yet my marriage broke up, and I became a stranger to my children. That was intellectual self-deception.

Over a much longer period of time I had been guilty of self-deception in my spiritual thinking. I was increasingly non-religious, believing in God but not in established religions. Then my mother died, and I realized how very important organized religion was to her and to the hundreds of millions of other people nearing the end of their lives on earth. If for no other reason than its value to the old, the sick, and the dependent young, established religions took on new importance to me in clear observation versus self-deception.

In retrospect I realized that nothing new had come into my world to educate me to overcome self-deception. As Aristotle said, "Most things are known: the trouble is that we do not apply what we know." That was my case, exactly. The information was there, but I was not letting it get into my own internal communication system. So pause for a moment and ask yourself about the major aspects of your life—your physical, intellectual, emotional, and spiritual life. Are you A) blocking off knowledge that is all around you and persisting in self-deception, or B) dumping false information into your internal communication system? Either or both are barriers to clear observation. You may have been misled, as I was, by the misinterpretation of the evolutionary process of perceiving as it was presented in the works of Darwin. My teachers convinced me that my sensory organs were developed primarily by adaptation to my needs. My eyesight, my hearing, and my senses of smell and touch were given as proof that I could *perceive things as they really were.* What I didn't learn until many years later was that stress could do things to my senses and make it impossible at times for me to see things as they really were. In effect, I had developed both a rejection process and an exclusion process. I could totally reject information critical of myself, or accept some and exclude other information given to me simultaneously. You might put this book down, close your eyes and breathe deeply for a few minutes, and ask yourself if you have a clear observation of yourself—or are you practicing a little, a moderate amount, or a lot of self-deception.

You may be amused in this connection by what we in the newspaper business called "the politicians optic," an exercise in self-deception that tells a great deal about the average politician. The governor of a large state was told there would be a reference to him in *Time Magazine.* He sent his assistant to the newstand to get a copy, looked hungrily at the index, turned the pages feverishly, and with shallow breathing and moist hands read the statement about himself. It said:

> Thomas Drool, the handsome, urbane, poetic and sometimes brilliant governor of the third largest state in the Union made the commencement address.

Governor Drool spat out a rude oath and roared, "What do they mean 'sometimes brilliant?'" This illustrates the exclusion process. Governor Drool excluded the very complimentary words—handsome, urbane, poetic, brilliant—and seized upon the qualifying "sometimes."

I will not belabor the point, but you might find this true story useful. At one point in my career I took over a business that had been run for decades by administrative-accounting types. The organization chart was a model worthy of the Harvard Business School. Every division, every department was shown in a box with lines running to the various points of authority and responsibility. It was all very neat, but the company was nearing bankruptcy for a variety of reasons, one of which was a bureaucratic paralysis because the president absolutely insisted on the rigid chain of command. When I realized what had happened I designed a communications chart for the daily running of the business, retaining the organization chart for administration and financial affairs. Several days after introducing the communications chart one of the best, young creative people came to me with the news that he had been about to quit because "I didn't come here to work in a goddamn box." He decided to stay because I had made him feel "visible."

There was an unexpected bonus for me as I switched from self-deception to clear observation. I became much more tolerant of other peoples' problems caused by their self-deception. There was one young executive who had enormous potential. But he had a habit that was irritating to me and potentially damaging to him. In almost any conversation about new developments he would invariably say "I know, I know" and literally cut off the flow of information. I didn't want to offend the man so I elected to get through to him by indirection. After considerable thought I evolved a formula that gave clear observation of the difference between *knowing* and *understanding*. His problem was that he actually did know a great deal about the business and his responsibility, but he didn't fully understand some of the long-term implications of what he knew. I created the following formulas which I had our art department print large and clear on artist display boards.

News + information + comment equals knowledge
Knowledge + reflection + feedback equals understanding

Understanding + commitment equals superiority ©

I made it a practice of controlling meetings without being dictatorial, so I was able to make my presentation without interruption. There were a dozen executives in the room, but I kept an eye on my target. I stressed the reflection and feedback quotients that convert knowledge into understanding and was pleased to see a very thoughtful look on the face of my young friend. Later, we had some private talks encouraged by the formulas, and his progress toward full realization of his potential accelerated.

One final point about self-deception. Human beings have been deceiving themselves for centuries that there were uncontrollable forces at work within each human being about which little could be done. There was a reference to "the beast within" that was used as an excuse for very bad behavior. To put this matter most simply, each human being has two systems operating in his marvelously complicated totality. There is one system over which we have quite good control and one that was thought to be beyond control. The latter is the combination of our gastrointestinal system (the stomach and intestines) and our cardiovascular system (the heart and the blood). Excellent research and applications have been done in Russia, Scandinavia, Germany, and the United States that prove that measures of control over these systems can be gained by self-regulation training of various types.

An outstanding example of this is practiced every day by actors and actresses on stage and in motion pictures. They use breathing, and the sounds related to breathing, as a major part of their acting. Consider the sharp intake of breath, the gasp, the cry, the shout. Actors and actresses can control their cardiovascular system, actually effecting physical changes. They can bring on tears, turn pale, assume muscular rigidity. If their pulses and the temperatures of their hands were measured, they would reflect the control these actors and actresses have as a result of their years of training and conditioning.

My plea to you as you leave this chapter is to persuade

yourself to overcome the self-deception that is part of almost everyone's makeup, and seek the clear observation that will help you get what you want out of life. There is a collective self-deception in America of total superiority over the poorer countries of the world because of our materialistic and technological advantages. We have about six percent of the world's population, but currently consume over thirty percent of the world's resources annually. Is it not self-deception to believe that as the world's population increases to seven, eight and nine billion people—most of them non-white—our country and the other Western industrial powers can continue the present policy of indifference?

Arnold Toynbee was one of the world's greatest persuaders. His "challenge and response" concept added a whole new dimension to the understanding of the failure of past civilizations and cultures to survive. Toward the end of his rich, full life he expressed the hope that our present civilization *might* survive if there was an interpenetration of the East and the West, for the salvation of both. It was his hope that the industrialized Western world would become more meditative and contemplative about the values of life and learn from the ancient world of the East, while the Eastern world would adopt some of the techniques and technologies of the West for the solution of its age-old problems of poverty, misery, ignorance, and disease. It is self-deception to believe that our civilization *must* survive; the record of history says otherwise. Very much to the point were the words George Bernard Shaw put in the mouth of his character Pra in "Simpleton of the Unexpected Isles:"

> Judgment is evaluation. Civilizations live by their evaluations. If the evaluations are false, the civilization perishes. We are not being punished, we are being evaluated.

That is how the civilization and acculturation of mankind began. Communication and persuasion have been absolutely fundamental to both. As the world became more populated and complicated, another aspect of persuasion appeared: compromise. Consider, as we go to the next chapter, the statement favored by Lenin, in our eyes perhaps, one of the world's evil persuaders. "In theoretical argument, never compromise." What he meant, and made a matter of practice, was to win all theoretical arguments by outshouting, outlasting, or outterrorizing opponents and those with varying viewpoints or ideas. This may work for a dictator, but it rarely does, in the long run, for most of us.

At the end of each chapter, where appropriate, I will promulgate what we will call the BDP Commandments. Here are the first three.

BDP Commandment 1 • **Overcome self-deception.**
BDP Commandment 2 • **Judgment is evaluation, not punishment.**
BDP Commandment 3 • **Compromise is a primary skill of persuasion.**

3

The Birth of a Persuader

★★★★★★★★★★★★★★★★★★★★★★★★★

A persuader is born at least twice, once literally and at least once allegorically. To whom a child is born can be extremely important to the nascent persuader, since some ethnic groups seemingly have qualities and characteristics that give them a head start in ordinary persuasion and high-level persuasion. Many Irish, for example, are said to be born with a "gift of gab." The Irish have institutionalized this characteristic by the veneration of the Blarney Stone. Visitors can, with some difficulty, and a little assistance, kiss the Blarney Stone, and lo and behold...

> There is a stone there/That whoever kisses
> Oh! he never misses/To grow eloquent,
> "Tis he may clamber/To a lady's chamber,
> Or become a member of Parliament."

It is generally true, I believe, that those groups known as "tribal people" have a facility with and a love of language. And those tribes such as the American Indians, the Jews, the black African, and the Irish—groups who have been persecuted and oppressed—seem to have depended on language and music as vital aids to survival. It is not strange; at times they had nothing else but words and music to express their faith and hope.

One of the most gifted Billion Dollar Persuaders from a tribal background is the incomparable Mel Brooks. There is absolutely no way to categorize him or his wild humor. It is three years since I saw his *Blazing Saddles*, but I can brighten any day by rolling around in my mind the delicious bit of business in this film that dealt with the brutal overseer of the western equivalent of a chain gang. Looking out over the gang of miserable, sweating, dusty blacks, he roars for a typical fieldhand song. The blacks respond with a beautifully harmonized version of "I Get No Kick From Champagne." Brooks could only have been born with that talent.

However, persuaders are also made as well as born. This started as a necessity around the time of the Industrial Revolution, when the natural gifts of salesmanship were inadequate to the task of explaining the advantages of technical equipment and systems to buyers. In less than eighty years there has been as great an advance in "sales engineering" as there has been in, say, manned flight. A whole new industry has grown—particularly in the United States—that is called *word processing*. It combines techniques and technology of the highest order. Its purpose is to persuade buyers of complicated equipment and systems that one producer's brand is better or best for the buyer's needs. The word processors can grind out enormous proposals—replete with schedules, graphs, and charts—that give the potential buyer the needed sense of support and security for his decision to buy. He reduces his risk, both literally and figuratively, by having documentation to support the claims of the seller.

Robert MacNamara carried the technique of documentation to great, perhaps even deceptive and dangerous lengths when he was Secretary of Defense. He was able to persuade President Lyndon Johnson, the Congress, parts of the press, and most of the American public that the United States was winning the war in Vietnam by showing monstrous documentation about enemy "body counts" and "villages pacified." I have had personal accounts of the "bulldozer" tactics of Robert MacNamara in meetings during which policy positions were to be decided by the president or the Security Council. MacNamara would arrive at the meeting with piles of reports, computer runouts, maps, graphs, and charts. At first, should MacNamara be challenged, he would dive into his documentation and overwhelm his opponents with a barrage of statistics. Gradually it was assumed that MacNamara *always* had the facts, and opposition to his ideas and plans melted. I cite this episode as a warning that there is evil persuasion in this troubled world, though such a warning is not necessary. My hope is that I can help readers recognize some of the early warning signs of evil persuasion.

John Fitzgerald Kennedy proved to be one of the most persuasive men on this earth. His father, Ambassador Joseph Kennedy, was also a persuasive man, but that fact has been obscured by fate, some personality flaws, and his enemies. In terms of fate, Joseph Kennedy was the victim of timing. He had the misfortune to be ambassador to England during the time Adolph Hitler rose to power and committed himself to the Thousand Year Third Reich, regardless of the cost. Joseph Kennedy was certain England and France could not stand alone against Germany, and he was right. He believed the United States should give aid to England, and he so recommended. But he was emotionally opposed to the involvement of the United States in the war in Europe. He believed the end result of our involvement would be the creation of a monstrous Communist enemy in Russia.

There are many descriptions of the Kennedy household during the years the eight children were born and raised in several large houses in Boston and Westchester County. There was constant talk, argument, storytelling, critiques, and much self-mockery and ironic ego-deflation. (This was the code of the Clan, and probably it was unchanged through a hundred generations.) Despite his early death, John Fitzgerald Kennedy persuaded the American people that they had to and could do better than they thought they could do. Stung by the startling success of the Russians with Sputnik, John Fitzgerald Kennedy persuaded the people of this country that *we should get to the moon within a decade.* We had to overcome the surprising lead of the Russians even if, as the joke went, "The Russians' captured German scientists were better than *our* captured German scientists."

I had two personal encounters with the late President Kennedy, both at the White House. One meeting was in the Oval Room, where the president sat and rocked in the world's most famous rocking chair chatting amiably with me about my life and my career in a sincere and interested manner. His appeal was total. He looked good; tall and slim, salt and pepper hair, that astounding voice with its Boston intonations. There was humor and warmth in those blue eyes, except when they turned steely in frustration and anger. The second meeting was on the third floor of the White House where the Kennedy family lived. He seemed even more gracious there, giving me a tour of the various rooms, particularly the Lincoln Room where he slept, alone, "because that telephone can ring at any hour."

John Fitzgerald Kennedy was a product of his home environment, a home described by our mutal friend Charles Spaulding as a family "moving in every direction and vitally involved and interested in what was going on. I had never seen any family like that.... I thought to myself 'this is really the best possible way to approach life.'" He seemed to be saying that in the Kennedy home all the senses were brought into full play, with a superabundance of talk a constant "cement" that tied this remarkable family together even through the most harrowing tragedies. John Kennedy, FDR, Adlai Stevenson, and the other great persuaders of our age were living evidence that language is truly the basic stuff of persuasion, and you, if a parent, can do nothing better for your family than to make your home a place where talk, argument, debate, and storytelling are constant. There are many opportunities outside the home for the development and exercise of verbal communication. School is the first opportunity. The budding social lives of children provide the next larger circle. Business and *pro bono publico* activities expand the opportunities even further.

Persuasion is divisible by two, in a very general sense. First, there is the *opportunity* to persuade, which is an administrative skill. Secondly, there is the *ability* to persuade, primarily a creative skill. The opportunity to persuade is compounded of several major elements. One is intelligent research. The persuader must find out in advance who has the authority to make an *affirmative* decision. In some very important situations where enormous amounts of money are involved, there may be some or many people who can say "no" and perhaps only one or two who can say "yes." The Billion Dollar Persuader knows that titles and appearances often lag behind true authority. I hope all aspiring persuaders are as lucky as I was in learning this vital lesson. It occurred when I was finishing my training as a salesmen for the Royal Typewriter Company in New York City. One of our assignments was to man the showroom into which an occasional buyer would come to purchase a typewriter, though rarely would it be an office model; showroom buyers were generally after portable typewriters. It seemed kind of a bore to the other trainees, but I enjoyed it. I was finishing with one professional writer who had bought a machine, when I noticed a shabbily dressed man with a weatherbeaten, seamed face enter the showroom and start looking at portable typewriters. One of the other trainees slipped out of the showroom and another stayed at his desk, studiously studying a brochure he had read dozens of time. The man moved around the room to the office machine section. I finished my transaction and dutifully walked over to the man, noticing immediately the odor of fish. It was so unexpected that I must have shown some reaction, and the man looked shyly at his clothes and shoes, saying softly, "I came from the boats." I gave him a big smile and asked how I could help him. He said, "My son and daughter are going off to school.... They say typewriters are helpful to kids...." I agreed, feeling a bit sorry for the man when he got the bad news about the cost of these portable typewriters, at that time about ninety dollars, each—a lot of money in 1939. He didn't bat an eyelash when I gave him the total price of the deluxe model, which he requested. He simply said, "Good, I'll take two," and took out a roll of bills, carried as sailors do, and peeled off the money. When he gave me his name and address, I realized that he *owned* a fleet of commercial fishing boats. Perhaps he wasn't a millionaire, but he would undoubtedly be a very rich man in time. That surprise made me much more sensitive to other aspects of first impressions.

Here's another case in point. I knew and played golf with the president of one of New York's largest banks. I had a computer-related program that I wanted to sell to his bank. He asked me to see his deputy, since the subject was computer technique and technology. I had my secretary call and make an appointment. I waited a very brief time for my host, who, I concluded, had sent one of his very young assistants to bring me to his office. The boyish, crew-cut "guide" led me to an enorm-ous office next to that of my friend, the president. He ushered me in, indicated a seat and then to my astonishment, went behind the desk and plopped himself down, put his feet on the huge desk, and said, "I'm very glad to meet you. I used to read about you in college." *He* was the deputy to the president and in charge of the electronic data processing and management in-formation system for the whole bank! I shuddered later about the consequences of a condescending attitude, if that were my nature. Fortunately it was not, and I benefited greatly from my refusal to take myself too seriously, although I took my respon-sibilities seriously indeed.

I never forgot that lesson, and was very sensitive to the fact that rising young men in business occupy smaller offices and bear lesser titles than the men they are moving to replace. Careful research before calls are made will often yield clues as to who can make affirmative decisions. The intelligent use of ex-pense accounts can be vital. It may be difficult to get a prospect to open up in a twenty-minute meeting in his office, but during a ninety-minute lunch the sensitive persuader can learn much about the intelligence, education, background, hopes, and aspirations of his luncheon guest. It is generally true that "the cream rises to the top" in most business organizations. So the well-dressed, courteous, articulate, and well-informed prospect will identify himself as a man on the way up.

Once the decision maker is identified, the next step is getting that person to agree to meet *under favorable circumstances*. It is not good enough to get a grudging agreement to meet. There is always a best way to approach this part of the opportunity-to-communicate equation. These are your available tools:

> The telephone, expertly used
> Letters and telegrams
> The secretary or executive secretary
> The administrative assistant, if any
> Unplanned meetings in social settings.
> Planned meetings in social settings.

I have found it generally true that the more confident the man or woman, the more accessible he or she is to a direct approach, by letter or telephone call, provided the persuader has adequate status, a well-known name or title.

Only rarely is it wise for a salesman, for example, to telephone or write to a president of a company that might be a prospective client. The president may be irritated, and the call may irritate the people down the line. This is particularly true in New York, Chicago, and Los Angeles, where companies have become rather bureaucratic. If the president is the man who will make the decision, then the salesman should go to his own management and have the initial call made by a high-level executive, perhaps even the president of his company. It wasn't at all unusual for Mr. Tom Watson of IBM to make a call on behalf of a salesman.

Once in a great while a daring exception pays off. When I first started making calls in Detroit I heard about a great man named Roger Keyes of General Motors. He was at the level just below the presidency of this gigantic company. His reputation was awesome. When something went awry at GM, and the normal procedure didn't work, Roger Keyes would be given the assignment to find out what the problem was. And invariably he would. I checked around the advertising circles and found that no media representative had *ever* seen Mr. Keyes. I decided to try. He came on the telephone immediately and, after a rather long pause, agreed to see me, though I could tell he had no idea what a media representative would be calling him about. He said, "You know, we have a very large advertising department." I assured him that I did know that, but said I was new to Detroit and wanted to get to know as much about it as possible. He sounded amused, then agreed.

I had severe misgivings when I walked into his reception room, to be coolly surveyed by his secretary, a handsome, gray-haired woman, to whom he had apparently communicated his amusement about my visit. There was some dread as I approached his desk. He unwound his very tall frame and greeted me. He had a massive dignity about him, heightened by his resemblance to Abe Lincoln. He asked, "What can I do for you, Mr. Culligan?"

I took a deep breath and said, "Mr. Keyes, I have heard that you are the greatest troubleshooter in General Motors. I'm kind of inclined that way for my future. There is no way to study that in school—how can a person prepare for that kind of career?"

The great, craggy face broke into a smile, and he started talking in a way that indicated that he had never been asked that question before, or, in fact, had given it much thought.

He explained that he had come up through the engineering route at GM. He felt that the single greatest talent of a good engineer was the ability to "factor" a problem, that is, take a large problem apart and look at aspects of it, then proceed to solve it in an orderly manner. He felt that engineers had a weakness, however, which he described as "engineering arrogance." They didn't always or often (and some never did) take into account some of the human elements of a large problem. I asked if he could give me an example. He thought for a moment, then told me about his most recent troubleshooting assignment.

After decades of improvement in the administrative areas of

GM—the vast area of paperwork including records, computer charts and tables, and financial records—something seemed to go wrong within the system. None of the department heads could figure it out, and top management became alarmed as the problem seemed to worsen. Roger Keyes was asked to dive into the situation. He did so and within six weeks had the most surprising answer for the president of GM. GM had used computers in many areas of their business for many years, and young and low-level people regularly used computers in their daily work as a matter of routine. The GM financial department became more and more aware of the great utility of computers—and the great increases in the cost of new computers. It was decided to get better control of the computers of the corporation and, theoretically, increase their effectiveness. A set of rules was promulgated, and schedules were set up for the access to the computers, with the financial department giving itself a priority position. All the little people down the line took offense at this. It struck at the self-esteem and dignity, so they simply slowed down and relaxed when the computers were not available to them. Roger Keyes made his report. A directive was issued to the financial department to cost justify computers for their own use and pay for their own. Within a month the General Motors administrative system was back in good order, and Roger Keyes had yet another decoration for his escutcheon.

No human being ever looked less like a salesman or persuader. What made Keyes one of the most effective problem solvers of his generation was common sense, compassion, and understanding the need of human beings for some visibility and dignity, regardless of their economic or educational levels. I commend that characteristic to you as you consider your own growth and development. Most psychologists and psychiatrists agree that the lack of self-esteem is a root cause for many juvenile and adult problems. Without human warmth, empathy, and understanding, effective persuasion is difficult if not impossible.

The persuader who is "made" also learns or is taught that

socializing and entertainment can be astonishingly effective in all aspects of life. Two examples may illustrate the point. I am a member of several clubs, both in the country and in the city. I was encouraged to learn to play golf early in my business life by several very successful older men. One of them, G. Harry Chamberlaine, proposed me for membership in the very exclusive Apawamis Country Club in Rye, New York. It was a bastion of old, Protestant, "establishment" Westchester. There was some chagrin and shock when the first Irishman, a Catholic, became a member four decades ago. By the time I became a member only a few eyebrows were raised. I did notice that there were closely knit groups within the club, and new members were often ignored for varying lengths of time. Apawamis was fortunate in having the best "locker man" I have met in any club in America, Frank Pasquale. Frank gradually assumed the role of matchmaker for the members who did not have regular foursomes. I told Frank to put new members into the groups with which I generally played. Over a twenty-year period I made dozens of new friends and acquaintances in this way; some of them became very good customers. It took very little effort on my part, but the dividends in friendship and business were huge. I look without admiration on the many club members whose expenses are paid by their businesses (ultimately their stockholders) who play golf only with old friends and employees of their companies, and do not give full value to their companies for this investment.

The second episode involved a mistake on my part. One of my New York clubs started out as a "men only" club, with a small room for ladies that had to be entered through a special route, away from the main entrance. The club, under pressure from a group of us, changed the policy, and women were permitted in all areas of the club. I invited an editor for lunch, expecting her to be impressed and enjoy the experience. I did not know that despite the beauty and femininity of this lady, she was an ardent feminist. That afternoon she was one of only four women among over a hundred, mainly portly, mainly impressive-looking business executives. She was first angry, then tense. After two drinks she told me why. To her, the club still looked and felt like a male chauvinist bastion. It was only after I told her that I was one of the leaders of the group that broke down the barriers that she seemed to relax.

The sensitive persuader should carefully consider the tricky chemistry of guest and meeting place. There are some people who are uneasy in very plush or sophisticated clubs or restaurants. There are others who think the "three martini lunch" is unconscionable waste (President Jimmy Carter, for one). One important buyer who has literally purchased millions of dollars of advertising from me over the years refused all offers of lunch. I learned from his secretary that he loved hot corned beef sandwiches on old-fashioned Jewish rye bread. I made a date to see him at 11:45 A.M. and entered with my attaché case filled with "deli" corned beef sandwiches. That became our pattern for years thereafter. He bought the products and services I presented to him right up to the month he retired.

The tax laws are changing, and entertainment expenses that have been deductable will no longer be so. Some club dues, yachts, and other such extravagances will no longer be paid for by corporations. As entertainment expenses are curtailed, a better use of those that are still permissable is a very serious responsibility of management.

In one corporation the president asked me to look over the entertainment situation not so much because of the large amount of money involved but from the viewpoint of its efficiency. I did a brief analysis and found that more than half the expense account luncheons were "staff lunches," that is, account executives having lunch with other company employees. Also, the same people were being entertained over and over again, with little demonstrable advantage to the company. However, we didn't want to have any repressive kind of restraints. I suggested the formation of The President's Luncheon Club, a plan in which account executives would be given the names of good prospects, with the hope that they would seek them out and take them to lunch. The program was remarkably successful in two ways. Account executives stopped having staff luncheons, and many new prospects were told about the company and its services. Several new business opportunities emerged from these Luncheon Club meetings, and the first new, million-dollar account paid for the entire expense of the concept for several years.

The importance of "being nice to be with" was forever etched in my psyche by one of the finest men it was my good fortune to meet during my early days in business. He was Howard Black, at that time executive vice president of Time, Inc. He had been persuaded to accept a job at Time when occasionally they didn't have enough money to pay equivalent salaries. Howard Black was compensated partly by Time, Inc. original stock. It made him a rich man. He was an extraordinarily good concept persuader, almost always in a very low key. He wanted to have me hired for the salesforce of *Life Magazine*, then becoming hugely successful. The advertising director was a man named Clay Buckout. He interviewed me and gave Howard Black a negative report; "too brash" was his comment. Howard Black told me about the report, and for the next decade we laughed a lot about Buckout's decision, as eventually I rose to the presidency of three companies, mainly on my ability to persuade. Fortunately for me, my ability eventually caught up with my brashness. It was during that discussion that I asked Howard Black how he went about making a decision on a new salesman. I remember putting to him the question, "What do you look for first?" His answer, so beautifully simple, was, "The first decision I make is, is the guy fun to be with." He went on to say, "Because if I don't like to be with him, why should my customers want to be with him?" The second quality Howard Black looked for was loyalty, not to him, but to the magazine and the company. When I got to the matter of intelligence, Howard Black said, "I always make sure to have a couple of nice dumb guys on the staff. Remember there are dumb buyers out there. The key is to try to match them."

As his friend, admirer, and student, I perceived that he was allegorically telling me something about sales and marketing management. I pressed him, and several drinks later he expressed his view that "there are no such things as bad salesmen, just bad sales managers." He made me understand, and I never forgot, that there was an enormous diversity of buyers. They were complicated human beings with their own fears, aspirations, and problems. The effective sales manager realized that, and had a diversified sales force, with close enough supervision to make some good matches of the right salesperson calling on the right buyer.

Here's a case in point. James M White was the second man to return from World War II hired by G. Harry Chamberlaine, advertising director of Good Housekeeping Magazine. Jim was a tall, sturdy Southern boy from Athens, Alabama. His Daddy had told him to "walk tall" in the big city, and Jim did, literally and figuratively. He became a great regional salesman for Good Housekeeping, but wanted more visability. He left Good Housekeeping and joined the staff of Life Magazine, where he established a fine record for salesmanship and a terrible record for writing sales reports. He then started a shopping column with a celebrity named Faye Emerson and did well financially for some years. I had the pleasure of hiring Jim as publisher of Holiday Magazine. Once again, in his unorthodox way, he did very well. Still restless, he left Holiday and acquired a small but beautifully targeted magazine called Promenade. Promenade was distributed only to the top luxury hotels in New York and thus completely avoided the onerous problems of distribution through newsstands and subscriptions. He narrowed his problems down to just two: editorial excellence and advertising sales. Jim had a favorite expression: "Most people don't do their work well anymore." He found the old type of salesman lazy and extravagant. He also noted the increase of women in the buying apparatus of the advertising agencies, so he started hiring women to sell his advertising. Today Promenade is one of the most successful small magazines in the country. Here again was a case of matching the salespersons to the characteristics of the buyers.

There were two comments about me in trade magazines while I was directing sales organizations. One was stated by a friend, the other by a critic. The first, which appeared in *Time*, was "Culligan is a tiger of a competitor." The second, uttered with a sneer, was "Culligan goes after an order like it was the Holy Grail." There was some truth in both opinions. I didn't try to get to know my competitors and I basically disliked them. They, I felt, were trying to take commission money away from me. I admit also to having some missionary zeal in persuading prospects to make decisions in my favor.

For example, when I worked for the Hearst organization, I sold space for *Good Housekeeping*. The magazine, along with two others, was on the media list of a large food company, one represented by a very good advertising agency. When the ad budget was cut by the company, the buyer removed *Woman's Home Companion* and retained *Good Housekeeping* and the *Ladies' Home Journal*. His explanation of why he kept *Good Housekeeping*—made to one of my superiors and later related to me—was: "My God, Culligan would make my life miserable if I knocked *Good Housekeeping* off the list." I knew why *Woman's Home Companion* got cut; its salesman was a nice guy who wouldn't complain. *Woman's Home Companion* later went out of business, a lesson not lost on me.

When the Curtis Publishing Company was looking for a new president, a board member was authorized to make recommendations. He called his favorite banker and asked him to check on my reputation. The banker asked a dozen or so of the bank's big customers in consumer products manufacturing about me. The consolidated report made to the director was laudatory. The first sentence read, "Culligan is one of the three best marketing men in the United States." When I was later shown the letter, I said, "What does he mean one of the *three* best? Who the hell is any better?" To be a Billion Dollar Persuader or a potential Billion Dollar Persuader, you need ego, *a lot* of ego. It is essential. I had enough for two. Make no mistake about this, ego and zeal are critically important qualities for the beginner in sales and marketing. There are frustrations and irritations that can, at times, be depressing. Such depression can negatively affect encounters and meetings while it lasts. Ego and zeal are antidotes.

Practical jokes are a fundamental part of any beginning experience. I was the victim of one in a part-time summer job as a junior salesman for the Royal Typewriter Company. The senior salesman told me to make a call on a small officer in a dreary building. When I gave the secretary my card, she seemed startled but dutifully took it into the office of her employer. She directed me to enter. As I did, the large, florid man was hoisting himself to full height. He bellowed, "When I die and go to hell, I'm going to take every goddammned Royal Typewriter salesman with me. Now get the hell out of my office." The senior salesman was waiting for me, bursting with mirth. That customer had gotten a "lemon," and in a comedy of errors in the service department, he had no satisfaction despite pleas that turned to agonized howls. The problem was finally resolved, but that customer was permanently disaffected.

Apart from the practical jokes my senior salesman was a fine fellow, but not overly ambitious. He worked just hard enough to stay out of trouble with the hard-driving sales manager whose greatest pleasure in life was to catch a group of his salesmen having coffee together at 9:30 A.M., in direct violation of his dictum, "In or on the way to a client's office by 9:15." He would sneak into the coffee shop, get as close as possible without detection, then rise to his full height and bellow the names of the offenders.

There was one moment of glory for me at Royal Typewriter. I noticed that my senior salesman did not direct me to one group of old buildings in one part of his territory. "Waste of time," he said. "They are all importers and exporters, holes-in-the-wall, crappy old antiques—they never buy."

I decided to look in one afternoon when I had had a good day placing demonstration units. It did seem a barren place, but I was well received by one gentleman who did all his business with European exporters to the United States. He had a very old machine, which my practiced eye detected had what was known as pica type, ten characters to the inch. There was a steady stream of correspondance with his clients, with postage being one of his heaviest items of expense. Suddenly an idea exploded. My company offered other type faces, one of which was called Super Elite and had fourteen characters to the inch. I asked his cooperation. We took out a typical file of copies of his overseas correspondance, and counted the words per line, then lines per page. By assuming fourteen characters to the inch versus ten to the inch, we came quickly to the forty percent saving in space. In some cases that improvement would enable the office to use one page rather than two. We related that to the saving in postage and calculated an annual saving that would offset the cost of a new typewriter in eighteen months. My host delightedly accepted my offer of a free demonstrator machine with Super Elite type. I fully expected a sale and should have closed the deal quickly. We got word from his office, however, to pick up the demonstrator. I went back to see the gentleman who proudly pointed to a *secondhand* typewriter with Super Elite type that he had gotten from the local office appliance store. "You were right," he chortled. "With this machine I get my money back in postage savings in *six* months." I was spared embarrassment back at the office by not biting on an unripe victory. I was not so fortunate a short time later.

The greatest embarrassment in my young life was also the result of a practical joke. My senior salesman assigned me to a small building, warning me that the combination elevator man and superintendant would not let me canvass the building if he saw me. He told me to simply watch the elevator leave the lobby, and then slip quickly up the fire exit stairs. I did that and raced up to the top floor of the building. There was a single door that was unlocked, so I walked through it, only to be confronted by an unusual sight. There were a dozen rows of desks, with about twenty desks per row, each occupied by a woman. Their backs were all to me. I could detect by their movements from the rear that they were manipulating or assembling something on the desk in front of them. At the far end of the room was a single desk facing the women. At that desk was a large man, his face wreathed in cigar smoke. I started in his direction, mentally preparing for the meeting. Then I heard the first giggle, then another, then a chorus of giggles, and finally a few outright laughs. I looked to my right and saw to my acute shock what the women were doing at these desks. *They were rolling condoms.* In the middle of each table was a phallus-shaped form. On one side was a box full of strung out condoms and a can of talcum powder. The women would pick up a condom, spread it over two fingers, and draw it down over the form. With the other hand, they would sprinkle some talcum powder on it, then with great artistry would roll the condom up into a ring and drop it into a box on the other side. They were all paid "piece work." Three young girls, walking up and down the aisles, would pick up the completed condoms, count them, and write the number on a slip and put the slip into the box. At the end of the day the slips would be presented to the boss for their daily wage. My red face and complete discomfiture was now showing. The boss, as I reached his desk, had an evil grin on his face. "Yeah, what can I do for ya?" The room became silent, as over a hundred women waited for their moment of triumph. I had to return the way I entered, past all those leering, sneering, laughing women who hadn't interrupted their condom rolling ritual for a second. One in particular, to the delight of her companions, grabbed the model phallus and made the classic "jerking off" motion, rolling her eyes heavenward. I fled down the stairs, past the startled elevator man to, once again, find my senior salesman convulsed with laughter. I learned that while zeal for a sale is essential, a minimum of research and preparation are always indicated before-the-fact.

The practical jokes did not always involve outsiders. One of the older salesmen was a most fastidious dresser who favored a pearl gray homburg. He was a bit of a stuffed shirt, so a logical target for the jokesters who didn't mind investing in a good laugh. The ringleader checked the size of the homburg, its order number, and the store that sold it. He collected money from the other participants and purchased two identical hats, one a quarter-size larger and one a quarter-size smaller. When the victim went to the men's room he switched hats putting the larger size on the rack in the morning, the smaller one on the rack in the afternoon, then the correct size in the evening. The victim went about with a perplexed frown for days. When the practical jokester tired of that, he rubbed a small amount of Limburger cheese on the sweat band of the original homburg. The perplexed frown turned to a disgusted scowl as the homburg wearer concluded that the whole world stank. I often thought of him to remind myself of an important principle of business: never assume "the facts" of your experience are immutable. Things can and almost always will change.

I started working at fourteen years of age in a summer resort on Long Island. My weekly contribution to the family coffers helped make our staying there possible. At first I was entrusted only with the delivery of groceries to the customers who didn't care to (or couldn't) carry home the large orders. The store manager was a profane, raucous old-country Irishman who was considered very desirable by some of the vacationing ladies. He would untie his apron ribbon once a day and leave the store with a wicked leer, saying, "Now *I'm* going to make a delivery."

At fourteen I was rather innocent and regularly horrified when I would overhear him say to an irate customer whose order had not been delivered on time, "Don't worry, ma'am, Matthew will have it into you in a minute." He'd hang up and laugh hysterically. He caused me to run into the back room of the store one day when he greeted an imposing customer with, "Well, you old bitch, what can I do for you today?" I didn't know at the time that she was deaf and hadn't learned lip-reading.

Although I was only the delivery boy, I was also occasionally assigned to help customers in the fresh vegetable department when things were very busy. I suspect that the manager thought I couldn't do much damage there. He was wrong. A customer wanted string beans; not having ever paid much attention to the many varieties of bean, I gave her lima beans. She came roaring back to the store a short time later and I very quickly had my first business defeat under my belt.

My "city kid" ignorance of things horticultural is best illustrated by what happened on one of my first weekends as a houseguest of the parents of a young lady on whom I had designs. Her mother was preparing dinner. She handed me a small knife and asked me to go out the kitchen door and bring back some chives. "They're in those clay pots," she advised. I came back with a handful of geraniums. Wrong pots!

The New York World's Fair in 1939 and 1940 broadened my horizons in many ways. My being hired gave me a surge of self-confidence since there were just twelve positions open and well over two hundred applicants for the jobs as guide-lecturers at the exhibit of the American Radiator–Standard Sanitary Company. Now I was propelled beyond one-on-one persuasion to group persuasion. The exhibit was excruciatingly dull, with boilers, hot water heaters, and air conditioning units standing mutely on raised islands. The esthetic effects were achieved by two open latticework walls of radiator pipes. I stood it as long as I could, then started making suggestions about livening up the exhibit. First they agreed to pipe in music. Then varicolored streamers of fabric were attached to the vents of the air conditioners. Their fluttering gaily was a good effect. The hardest change to get approval on was a demonstration of water being changed to steam in a boiler chamber, behind protective glass. After several months it was done, and attracted attention. Every day was a learning experience for me, both on and off the job. Every good salesperson knows instinctively that even a dull subject can be made more interesting by color, sound, and movement.

On the Fair's midway there was a bewildering variety of bars and restaurants, sideshows, freak shows, nude shows, and carnival rides. I went alone the first time, drifting delightedly along, drinking in the sights, sounds, and smells. I perked up when I heard, penetrating through the cacaphony, a young, brassy male voice describing, "Lulu, she walks, talks, juggles forks, eats corks, and crawls on her belly like a reptile." The voice drew me like a magnet to the fringe of the crowd, drawn in a semicircle around a raised wooden platform. On it was a girl, dressed in a harem costume, veiled below the eyes. Her ample bosom protruded and jiggled around as she rotated her hips and shoulders. That was Lulu, a striptease artist. The outrageous exhortation was delivered by a strapping young, red-haired man, most obviously Irish.

He was rounding up the group of Lulu's next performance in the centuries-old mode of the sideshow barker. He extended his spiel: "Step right up, ladies and gentlemen! Meet *Lulu!* She balks, stalks, walks, talks, eats corks, juggles forks, and crawls on her belly like a reptile." He was attired in the traditional garb of the midway barker: striped shirt with black elastic arm bands, bow tie, and straw hat with a red, white, and blue band. I looked past the outfit to the face. "By God," I said to myself, "*I know him.*"

In a flash, I recalled the circumstances, but not the name. He had been a competitive grocery store delivery boy at Rockaway Beach. While I had worked for Daniel Reeves, he was at the A&P half a block away. We both pushed carts full of boxes filled with groceries. I'd never spoken to him, but we'd exchanged friendly grins and waves.

I waited until he finished his spiel, stopped him, and reminded him of our past. He also remembered. He said, "Christ, I'm thirsty. Let's have a beer."

Thus began my first ramble into the wonderful world of show business. My friend Kevin Molloy was an incomparable guide to the great joints and lovely, willing ladies of the midway. I soon forgot the girls at our exhibit, the guides who swung their shapely bottoms all over the fairgrounds, and the "stews" (airline hostesses who lived all over the county of Queens).

I also made an astonishing alliance with Lulu. From sheer exhaustion (at twenty, that's sheer) I settled, literally and figuratively, on a girl who worked in the only really nude show. It wasn't closed down because the audience viewed the dozen girls through reverse telescopes. Appearing less than a foot high, they were positively chaste in appearance, even though they were supposed to be Amazon women between battles. Fate or the luck of the Irish gave me this interlude just before the United States entered World War II.

The marvelous memories and the new skills of group persuasion made my advancement in the army very rapid. I qualified for what was known as the Volunteer Officers Program in which men with deferments could volunteer and perhaps qualify for commissions. I was temporarily deferred because of my older brother and younger sister being in the service, he as a colonel in Psychological Warfare and she as a first lieutenant in the Army Medical Corps.

I ranked number two in my class at Fort Benning, coming out of the pack quickly because of a stentorian voice for close order drill and the ability (developed at the World's Fair) to think on my feet and speak clearly and well to groups.

When the war ended, fate again took a hand . At a bar on 52nd Street in New York, while still in uniform, I met a most gracious gentleman who reacted to the patch on my left eye and bandaged left wrist, which for comfort I carried in a sling. Through him I secured my first full-time career job as a salesman with *Good Housekeeping Magazine*. I advanced rapidly to head of the home building department, coming to the attention of the president of the Hearst Corporation by two notable achievements: the first schedule of advertising from an airline in a woman's magazine, and a neat trick called *"The Fifty Best Homes from Good Housekeeping."*

Here again, I don't know just how the idea developed. *Good Housekeeping* commissioned leading architects to design original houses for its monthly editorials. After three years there were a total of nearly one hundred drawings of charming homes, with details on landscaping and outdoor notions. *Good Housekeeping* owned these drawings, which were gathering dust in the files. I presented a plan to offer the fifty best of these in a large coffee table-sized book, knowing that at any given time a certain percentage of people were considering building new homes. There was no investment initially, since the book would be offered in the pages of *Good Housekeeping Magazine* at the cost only of paper and ink. I suggested we charge twenty-five dollars for the book. One of my critics asked, "Why twenty five dollars?" "Because that is half of fifty dollars," I replied. He never did become a fan.

I badly underestimated the appeal of a *The Fifty Best Homes From Good Housekeeping*. The orders poured in with checks and money orders, making the whole operation self-financing.

There was some minor expense in advising buyers that there would be a delay in their receipt of the book because of unprecedented demand. That experience, which propelled me toward management recognition, caused me to resolve that I would always, repeat *always*, look for facts or resources that had been ignored or overlooked by others. I believe I could have gone to the top of the Hearst Corporation, but the lure of television was irresistible.

My first assignment at NBC was "The Today Show" with Dave Garroway.

It could have been a disaster, for "The Today Show" had not "changed the viewing habits of America," as one overzealous promotion man trumpeted. In fact, the ratings of "The Today Show" started out anemic, and, after the first blush of publicity and newspaper and on-the air promotion, they trailed off to near nothingness on a national basis. It was losing money at the rate of $1.7 million a year, with a dismal trend in its advertising income. I would like very much to say that my appearance made a difference. It didn't. That is, my appearance alone did not cause much excitement either internally or externally. But almost simultaneously with my entering the picture, my two associates, Dick Pinkham and Mort Werner (executive producer and producer respectively), walked into their reception room and were startled by the sight of a young chimpanzee sitting between its two young owners. This was to become the best known simian in the United States.

Only King Kong outdistanced J. Fred Muggs on a worldwide basis. Pinkham and Werner, divinely inspired, hired J. Fred Muggs, and made him a co-star with Dave Garroway who, in the interest of the survival of the show, entered into an uneasy alliance with the monkey. The press, bored stiff with "Today," reacted with high glee to J. Fred Muggs and hundreds of thousands of lines of publicity and thousands of pictures of Muggs appeared in all the newspapers of the country. Men and women, many forced to turn on "Today" by their screaming children, appreciated the novelty of J. Fred Muggs, but also noted that "The Today Show" had improved greatly, with

Dave Garroway completely at ease with the medium and the time of day. I was able to take the new publicity and the improved ratings to the advertising agencies. In some meetings I took Dave Garroway with me and marvelled at his poise and sly good humor. J. Fred Muggs came to other meetings and was an immediate hit.

The "Today" chimpanzee did more than get an increase in ratings. It enabled me to completely change the marketing ambiance of "The Today Show" from an overpublicized, electronicly gimmicked program to a personality array where, guided by Dave Garroway, viewers could be gently entertained as well as informed. The aspiring Billion Dollar Persuader should have as one of his major commandments Thou Shalt Not Oversell. The smart-alecks in the press and among the competition dearly love to use ridicule against the man or woman who tries to do something different. The original promoters of "The Today Show" made the fatal error of claiming far too much for a program between 7:00 and 9:00 A.M. When they failed to deliver on their pretentious claims they were lambasted. The press reports on the new "Today" with J. Fred Muggs renewed interest in the show, and the influence of Dave Garroway made the offering ideal for that time of the morning.

I persuaded advertisers that, despite early bad reviews, "Today" would succeed; I convinced enough of them, in fact, that there was sufficient revenue to ensure the show's continued existence while the bugs in its format were worked out. Shortly thereafter, I and my staff at NBC sold out both "The Tonight Show" and "Home" before or shortly after they debuted on television.

During my tenure as the head of the NBC Radio Network in the late 1950s, I succeeded in persuading advertisers to increase their radio budgets when they were disenchanted with radio and only wanted to advertise on television. I did my job so well that during my second year, there was one quarter in which the gross profits of NBC Radio surpassed those of NBC Television!

My greatest coup in business, however, came in 1962 when I was offered the presidency of the giant Curtis Publishing

Company. As is so often the case, I knew that if I accepted the job, it was a chance for me to succeed brilliantly or to fail spectacularly. I think it is worth presenting in some detail because it shows dramatically what the power of persuasion can achieve and, further, it illustrates many of the elements to be discussed later in this book.

Before accepting the job at Curtis, I investigated the situation. What I found was the following:

1. The company was ninety days from bankruptcy. It owed four banks a total of $22 million dollars and, if payment were demanded, it couldn't pay without liquidating the business through filing for bankruptcy.
2. The company's management had been discredited and had collapsed. The president had been fired while traveling in Europe. The employees were demoralized and dispirited; they were near despair.
3. The board of directors was terrified that the company was going to collapse. It had offered me the job on the basis of my record of achievement and my reputation for somehow succeeding when all seemed lost.

It was not an encouraging picture, to say the least. On the other hand, my rapid appraisal of the situation revealed the following positive elements:

1. The Curtis banks would be very vulnerable if the company was forced into bankruptcy because of their own incredible lack of diligence in monitoring the company's financial position. This, I felt, would force them to give me time.
2. *The Saturday Evening Post* had an enormous residue of good will with the executives of the U.S. business community, as did Curtis itself being one of America's older large companies; the other Curtis magazines (*Ladies' Home Journal, Holiday, American Home,* and *Jack and Jill*) were also respected publications.
3. The Curtis "family" of employees—editors, production

people, artists, writers, salesmen—were basically a good group who could, with vigorous leadership, be reinspired.

The Curtis director who had been appointed "a committee of one" to persuade me to take the job was Milton Gould, a very smart, streetwise New York lawyer of bone-crushing aggressiveness. He could be calmly persuasive when he wanted to be. That was his technique with me. When I was still wavering and listed the negatives of the job, he said, "Right, but those are all the reasons I can get the Curtis board to give you everything you demand. Win, lose, or draw, you'll come out of there with a million dollars." But when Milton Gould couldn't get what he wanted with sweet reasonableness, he turned tough and threatening. When the board of directors hesitated to vote to fire the former president, he reportedly said, "Gentlemen, if this action is not taken *now*, I am going back to New York and file a class action suit against this board for failing in its fiduciary responsibility to the shareholders." The Philadelphia directors passed the resolution to remove the president, and Milton Gould, for a month or so, was in the power seat of this $600 million corporation. I watched him operate with a sense of awe and unease. This man, I concluded, would be a very difficult enemy, since as a lawyer he operated from a very privileged posture. He did wedge me into the presidency of the Curtis Publishing Company after getting agreement from the board that my compensation package would literally be worth a million dollars to me if I stayed for the full five years of my contract. He did become my corporate enemy several years later and struck me some heavy blows during a take-over attempt by a former client of his and some Wall Street corporate raiders. I learned that any chief executive officer of a troubled company could be brought down by rumor, slander, exaggeration, and distortion. I learned the meaning of the description "undertaker" as applied to lawyers.

A more experienced, more cautious executive would, I think, have still rejected the job; the negatives did seem to outweigh the positives. I, nevertheless, decided otherwise. With the double portion of ego that I had and the very scale of the challenge as motivation, I accepted.

Previous to my arrival at the Philadelphia headquarters of Curtis in July 1962, I had learned that large problems are best attacked with large action programs and not with public relations puffery. I made my plans rapidly but not so rapidly that they were flawed.

In the first phase of my master plan, I announced a national sales blitz that would take me into the offices of the presidents of the two hundred largest corporation in the United States within a period of six months. That had never been attempted before. The national sales force of Curtis was given specific instructions and schedules for my arrival in each territory. The larger advertising agencies were asked to see me first so that I could inform them of what I would explain and show their clients.

Next, I asked Robert Sherrod, editor of *The Saturday Evening Post*, to get me an appointment with President John F. Kennedy, assuming that my account of such a meeting would give me an effective opening for my presentations with advertising agencies, but only with selected top management of *client* organizations. The reason was simple. Most of the young, liberal people in advertising agencies would welcome and respond to my stories about President John Fitzgerald Kennedy, whom many idolized. Most businessmen were staunch Republicans who either knew or suspected that President Kennedy was not a rabid fan of businessmen. For meetings with conservative businessmen I used the Curtis commitment to competitive enterprise as my "warmer-upper."

It is vitally important to the aspiring persuader to learn how to warm up an audience before getting into the serious business of persuading. Laughter has a marvelous ability to open up the mind of a prospect. If he laughs at your jokes he is, in a way, saying "yes." When I had my two "warmer-uppers" ready, I took the next giant step: the development of a specific presentation for each kind of meeting. I had learned in previous years that almost any presentation could be preordained to failure if it did not take into account the nature of the audience, the time of day, the size of the room, interferences, and distractions. Three experiences concerning this come immediately to mind.

One was at Mount Pleasant, Iowa, where I went to make the commencement address at Iowa Wesleyan College. It was a perfect day for a commencement with clear cloudless skies and a breeze whipping the flags and the flowing academic gowns of the assembled men and women. I was announced and introduced in a manner usually reserved for obituaries. The audience reacted with excitement to this one-eyed Irish Catholic, the only one in Mount Pleasant. My address, entitled "The Suicide of the Competitive Enterprise System," seemed to be going over very well. I had a conclusion that fell just a little short of "what doth it profit a man if he gain the whole world and suffer the loss of his soul?" But just as I was about to inflict it on my audience, I heard a rumbling on my left that got louder and louder with each second. The audience reacted, I paused, and we all looked to the left as around the bend came a freight train of over thirty cars pulled by a heavily puffing locomotive. The noise was deafening. I concluded it was useless to compete, so I made the most of the situation. I waved at the engineer. The faculty on stage with me laughed, then *they* waved at the engineer. The graduating students rose, turned, and they, too, waved to the engineer. I finished the speech to good applause, then turned to Dr. Hasselmeyer, the dean, to find him grinning wickedly at me. That particular train was a regularly scheduled one, which had been interrupting commencement exercises for decades. I had passed the test. But I remembered.

The second episode happened in St. Louis, during a presentation I was making to a luncheon audience. We were in a new, large, very efficent motel. What hadn't been noted by my advance man who made the arrangements was that the room we had was partitioned by a sliding wall that was not soundproofed. Shortly after I was introduced and started my presentation, the group in the next area sang "My Country 'Tis of Thee" then the MC ripped off a series of one-liners that convulsed *his* audience. Our meeting was a disaster. I remembered.

The third experience was bitter, but the bitterness was some-what relieved by the knowledge that I was outsmarted by one of the brightest men in the advertising business, Rodney Erickson of Young and Rubicam. At the time I was president of the NBC Radio Network (and executive vice president of NBC overall). Television was in its heyday, with advertisers flocking to it—to the discouragement and despair of other media. The most seriously hit was network radio. I had invented a concept called "imagery transfer." Admittedly it was an invention of necessity, almost desperation, but it was an achievement of which I was and am very proud. It was concept persuasion (Chapter Five) of the highest order. It not only achieved its aim in its time and context, but it survived to the present day. It became the basis for the majority of radio commercials, even though the name imagery transfer is no longer used.

I quote here the story by Jo Ransom, of *Variety*.

WHILE OTHERS PUSH PANIC BUTTON
CULLIGAN STEERS NBC RADIO
INTO NEW VISTAS AS AM'S TORCHBEARER

Since the recent ominous announcement of CBS Radio's barter system with its affiliates, the NBC Radio Network has racked up some 16 succulent orders, including renewals for a total amount of more than $2,700,000 in net revenue.

NBC now regards itself as undisputed network radio leader in the land. Two years ago it was looked upon as third in ratings, fourth in sponsored hours, and third in clearances. It was unde-niable third in prestige in those days. Credited with restoring NBC Radio to its present preeminent role is Matthew J. Culligan, NBC veep in charge of the radio network.

Undoubtedly his most talked-about contribution has been the concept of "Imagery Transfer" by which major American adver-tisers keep alive, by skillfully placed low-cost radio commercials, "the mental images they have created in the public mind at great cost through the visual media."

The full story of imagery transfer and NBC News-on-the-

Hour, which netted NBC hundreds of millions of dollars in new revenues, is told later. My point in citing it briefly here relates to the importance of advance planning of presentations, of taking *all* things into account. I made an immediate sale of imagery transfer to a top executive of Johnson & Johnson, going over the head of their advertising agency, Young and Rubicam, then gung ho on using television for this client. Bob Johnson, the head of the division involved at his company (dominated by his father, General Johnson) was captivated by my presentation, which was carefully designed for a small, intimate setting, dimly lit, with superb sound equipment. We sat around a table, had coffee, and in a very low-key manner I explained in quasi-scientific lingo the demand impulse theory, closure, and other aspects of the gestalt theory. My audience, including my own associates, looked a bit stunned. But then the demonstration started, and it was a complete triumph. By the careful selection of full-page, color magazine ads, and TV commercials, I established the mental "picture" of the product and its advantages. Then on signal, the lights went out, and we played a series of fifteen-second audio commercials that caused a recall of the mental pictures. It was uncanny—and uncannily effective. When the lights went up, I *knew* we had Bob Johnson. Rodney Erickson, who was there representing the advertising agency, knew it also, but he was much too smart to swim against the tide. He said, "Very interesting... very interesting." Bob Johnson asked for a proposal. We had one ready and handed out copies asking for a budget of $2 million for *radio*. Rod Erickson looked at me in disbelief, but Bob Johnson nodded affirmatively, then he asked Erickson, "Well, what about it?" Erickson promised an agency evaluation immediately and effectively ended the meeting. I should have left town for a week or two, but I didn't.

Within two days I got the invitation to repeat the presentation to Bob Johnson and to the account and media and broadcasting people at Young and Rubicam, and was told that they would supply all the necessary equipment and a conference room. I knew well the quality of their audio equipment and the attractiveness of their conference rooms. It never occured to me to send a representative to the agency to check on the facilities. When I arrived for the presentation I found myself in a screening room with a podium. The setting was entirely right for a television presentation and absolutely wrong for radio. I looked at Rod Erickson. He rolled his eyes innocently heavenward, but couldn't restrain a grin. My presentation went over like a lead balloon. Bob Johnson looked at me with dismay. The Johnson & Johnson budget stayed in daytime television. But, without emnity to Rod Erickson, who is still a friend, I remembered.

That and other lessons of the past were very much in mind when I planned the national sales blitz for Curtis Publishing. It was a multipurpose campaign, with internal objectives as well as sales. It was a morale booster for the previously dispirited people of Curtis. It energized the entire sales force who were determined to clean up their acts by the time I blew into town.

Great pains were taken with the various presentations that would be made. There would be specially crafted appeals for one-on-one, small groups, and breakfast, luncheon, and dinner meetings. My public relations expert developed a dozen or so anecdotal stories calculated to keep the name of the *Post* and me in circulation on at least a weekly basis. Finally, in each major city, my former NBC affiliates were told of my arrival in order to stimulate radio and television interviews that would supplement the newspaper coverage of my visit. And each presentation room was carefully checked.

In the second phase, the execution of the plan, I used commercial airlines for trips of over a thousand miles and the company's small twin-engine plane for shorter trips. The little Curtis helicopter was used in some cities for darting trips to big companies in remote places like Racine, Wisconsin. The effect of landing on a corporation's lawn (with permission, of course) was magical.

Each presentation had one theme: the United States needs *The Saturday Evening Post*. Variations were programed into the presentation according to each prospect's need, always *his* need. I finished each with an emotional appeal that went something like this: "Sir, your advertising agency is one of the very best in the United States. It is spending *your* money prudently and most efficiently. At the moment, the *Post* may not be the perfect buy for your advertising—but I can promise you it soon will be. So, I appeal to you as one head of business to another, give the *Post* some help now and we'll make it up to you in the future."

No one had ever made such an appeal before. Many of the company presidents responded. (One acted the moment I left his office by calling his ad managers and telling them to get ads into the *Post*.) The program worked; in some cases it worked too well and some ad managers and ad agencies resented my over-their-heads approach. But the situation was desperate and only desperate measures could have worked in the narrow time-frame available to me.

In that six-month sales blitz, I brought in $78 million in advertising contracts. That was, of course, a critically important objective to have achieved, but the other, multilevel effects of it were momentous:

1. The Curtis banks, when they saw me make good on my promises (a successful sales blitz plus massive cost reductions) increased our credit-line from $22 to $26 million.
2. Employee morale surged upward.
3. Curtis common stock prices moved upward and, interestingly, advertising in the other Curtis magazines increased dramatically. The *Post*, the flagship of Curtis, had drawn the other magazines along.
4. Most importantly, the country's greatest banker, Serge Semenenko, agreed, when he saw me deliver on my promises, to make his the lead bank in a new $38 million credit for Curtis.

All values considered, my persuasion blitz had, in six months, brought in over a hundred million dollars. Meeting and getting to know Serge Semenenko was a monumental dividend, for he was a Billion Dollar Persuader and the best banker in the United States, in my opinion. He was an immigrant child from Russia, with a finely honed mind and a superb instinct for dependable people. He was courtesy personified; he never raised his voice, and he radiated authority and influence, using his surroundings with the skill of a Broadway stage director. He occupied a floor at the elegant Pierre Hotel on Fifth Avenue in New York City. He always employed a beautiful woman as his executive secretary. When one entered the office part of the floor, the greeting was most gracious. Serge Semenenko had a steady stream of visitors and had a traffic pattern that enabled him to give everybody an adequate opportunity to speak his mind without any later visitor feeling that he was being unduly delayed. A few minutes with the executive secretary, and the visitor was ushered into a small conference room. On first meetings Serge Semenenko would come to that room for the meeting. The next visitor might be taken into Serge Semenenko's office, where waiting was a pleasure, refreshments being offered. Other visitors were taken to his apartment, a magnificently furnished suite where, again, refreshments would be offered. In dozens of meetings with Serge Semenenko I was never kept waiting for more than ten minutes, and these literally flew by because of the courteous manner of his staff.

Serge also had a beautiful home in Boston, on famed River Street, with a beautiful view of the Charles River. A few of his friends were invited there. A very choice few would be given the ultimate treat, a cruise on the two-hundred-twelve-foot yacht that the bank leased for Semenenko for ten weeks each summer and fall. The yacht, the *Shemara*, was the second biggest boat in the English registry, the biggest being the yacht of the British royal family. The *Shemara* had a crew of thirty-two, an extraordinary chef and a guest list to cause elation and wonder. On one cruise there was Miss Italy, Miss Greece, and two starlets from the Venice Film Festival. It was on this yacht that I participated in one of the greatest feats of persuasion in history, the persuasion via ship's telephone of seven bankers to join a $38 million credit for Curtis Publishing, which during the previous year had been a prime candidate for bankruptcy!

Serge Semenenko never drank alcololic beverages (except at his daughter's sixteenth birthday party) and I found out why.

Serge did business all around the world via telephone. It was not unusual for him to be called from the dinner table, or from the salon as midnight, or from bed at any time of the morning, to discuss million-dollar deals. He would not take the chance of being unclear or indecisive, so he was always cold sober.

We had one meeting on board the yacht at which he made a commitment for the First National Bank of Boston, for $10 million. He said this was psychologically important. His bank would have the biggest individual portion. He would not suggest that any other bank come in for more than $7.5 million. He then gave instructions to his radio operator to place calls to the banks he had in mind to join the consortium. He told me to advise the steward where I was at all times, so that I could join him as the calls came through. He followed the same pattern in each call. He would say, "This is Serge Semenenko calling. I have decided to enter the Curtis situation. The First National Bank of Boston has committed $10 million to a total credit of $38 million. I would be delighted to have your bank participate for up to $7,500,000." He would then listen for a while, answer questions, and in every conversation he would say, "There is more than adequate net queek." I had never heard the expression before. I learned that *net queek* was actually net quick in his Russian accent! To the bankers on the other end of the line that meant that if Curtis went down, there were assets enough for the banks to get their full loans repaid, since the obligations of Curtis would be first to the employees in salaries, then to the banks.

The deals were not made on the telephone, for obvious reasons. Serge would put me on the telephone where, after some pleasantries, the banker would express interest in joining the group. Then we would set up a date for my visit when I returned to the United States. It took me less than thirty days to get the commitments from the six other banks, one in Texas, one in Los Angeles, three in Philadelphia, and one in New York. I had one moment of near panic when Pat Clifford, the president of the Franklin National Bank, seemed about to pull out at our second meeting. He said, "I know I said Franklin would come in for $3.5. I was wrong." He took a long pause while I stopped breathing, then said, "The board approved $5 million," putting his hand out with a great smile on his handsome face.

I have presented much, perhaps too much, about money as a reward for persuasion. Also, many of my examples have included businessmen and marketing executives and salesmen. These are purely illustrations of attitudes and abilities of people with whom I have come in close contact.

There was one fine human being who could have been a Billion Dollar Persuader in business, but he chose instead to use his abilities to help young people. He became an official of the Boy Scouts of America, at a modest salary. He persuaded me to help the Boy Scouts in the one way I could: raising money for that organization. I was terribly busy at the time, making my way up the success ladder. I tried to decline on that basis. He looked at me sadly and said, "I'm busy, too, trying to help these kids. I've learned that if we are to get this job done we must get help from the busiest people around. Please." I found him irresistible, and for a decade or so, I plunged into the annual campaign and set some kind of record for money raised. In one case we got half a million people to come to a Boy Scout Jamboree at the Coliseum on Columbus Circle, New York. But before that could be done, I had to accomplish a near miracle in persuasion with the dozen or so unions whose cooperation and assistance was necessary. Labor management problems were very severe at the time, and I was warned that the unions would laugh in my face if I asked them to provide services for nothing and permit volunteer workers to come into their domain. I met them one by one, told them what was at stake, and they agreed. I then got Bob Sarnoff, the president of NBC, to become chairman of the Jamboree, a spot that attracted much publicity, knowing that he would get the NBC news department to give adequate coverage to the event and swell the attendance. Being involved in the event showed that the greatest of satisfactions can come from doing something for those who need help or are less fortunate.

Those opportunies are available to you, too, no matter what your field.

My most unusual fund-raising activity, however, was for the United Jewish Appeal. Having grown up in a neighborhood that had many Jewish families, I identified early with the Jewish cause in Israel. Many Irish did, and to this day, the Irish are very well received in Israel by the older Jews who knew some of the Iris flyers, officers, and soldiers who joined the Israeli forces from time to time. Some are even buried there. A very good friend asked me to consider becoming co-chairman of the magazine division of the UJA. I accepted this challenge, and raised a record amount of money from the magazine industry. The shock value of having an Irish Catholic as co-chairman of a United Jewish Appeal campaign was a major factor, I'm sure, in our success.

The rest of this chapter deals with the persuaders who are made. Primary among this group are the so-called sales engineers who became necessary in the marketing complex because of the increasing sophistication of products and services, and the greater implications of failure for the buyer. If a huge, expensive piece of equipment failed, the losses could run into the hundreds of thousands—or even millions—of dollars. Personality, entertainment, smooth conversation, and presentation skills are relatively unimportant. In this area, intelligence, competence, and training are the key ingredients. Very often the meetings of salesman and buyer are exactly the same as meetings of engineers. What was the need? Could the need be factored readily? What was the solution? What were the products and services available to reach the solution?

Mr. Thomas Watson, the builder of IBM, must rank among the very top on anybody's list of Billion Dollar Persuaders. The IBM marketing operation is, in my judgment, the best in heavy goods industry in the world. It is truly incomparable, a fact that has been learned to the deep regret of such companies as RCA and General Electric who elected to challange IBM on its own turf: the computer industry. RCA made two basic mistakes. They thought they could launch a full line of computers against IBM, and they thought that money could buy a marketing organization to compete with IBM. There is literally not enough money in any American company to build an organization that can compete with IBM on a short-term basis. Of course, a company with unlimited funds and a great deal of energy and time could, by hiring away IBM sales managers and salesmen, build up an organization that would, on paper, look comparable to IBM. But that simply couldn't work. The IBM marketing system is an extraordinary interrelationship of exceptional people, marvelous training and stimulation, pride and discipline. IBM literally "makes" great persuaders out of men and women who can enter their marketing operations from almost any source. An IBM marketing man is expected to call for backup when threatened with the loss of a piece of business. He can never be fired for losing a client if he has "fired all the shots" which, in the old days, included calling for top management help, and that might turn out to be one of the Watson family! I admit to using this characteristic of IBM when I faced my first major crisis involving computers. Less than a month after taking over a major corporation that completed seven *billion* transactions a year, the arrogant head of the computer operation demanded to see me. He knew I did not have extensive experience in computer operations. He said, "Mr. Culligan, if we do not spend two million dollars for new equipment *now*, we will have a major disaster on our hands." There was one major problem; the company *did not have* two million dollars to commit or spend, but how was I to know whether his statement was accurate? I told him I'd let him know, locked my office door, and asked myself the question, *How can I get the quickest education on computers in American history?* My company had three IBM 1401 computers. We were one of the biggest computer customers for IBM in Philadelphia. I called RCA and told them I would welcome a presentation from them on replacement of our IBM computers with RCA units. They practically salivated and promised to make a presentation within a week. I sent word to the IBM management that RCA was making a presentation for our business. Their response was immediate. "Give us an opportunity to defend our system and program the next generation of equipment." A presentation date was given to them, the day after the RCA presentation. Ruthless tactics on my part? Yes, certainly, but my situation was desperate. IBM had enjoyed and profited from our business for more than a decade. RCA was hungry for our business. The back-to-back presentations of these two vigorous competitors gave me the quickest possible education in computer equipment. They were attended by not only the head of our computer operation, but also by his senior staff members. The head of operations became much more respectful for the duration of his employment—which was not long. In a strange way he helped me, for then I determined never to be at the mercy of a subordinate because of ignorance of electronics and abhorrence of mathematics. When business conditions improved, and money did become available for modernization of our computer operations, I made further enquiries about computer *leasing*. I was able to go to the board of directors and the lending banks (who had approval for all major investments) persuade them to approve a comprehensive plan for a combination of computer leasing and some acquisitions that actually improved the balance sheet. A lesson for aspiring Billion Dollar Persuaders: learn to make a virtue of necessity.

During the late 1960s I received an invitation to be principal speaker at the International Marketing Conference in San Francisco. The invitation itself was most flattering, since this was the most prestigious organization of its kind in the world. I decided to make the most of my opportunity, so I developed a speech that I called "Computer Applications to Marketing." I was astounded by the reaction to the speech, both in San Francisco and nationally. Hundreds of copies were requested by the participants at the meeting. The most flattering reaction was a request by General Foods for the right to reprint it for their Critical Papers Program. Fred Lambrou, the head of both EDP and Management Information Systems of General Foods had helped me in the preparation of my speech, so I was delighted to agree. In that speech, for the first time in U.S. history, the thirty-seven different computer applications to marketing were presented to the international marketing executives of the world's great corporations. The speech did wonders for my personal credibility for the next decade.

Public speaking is a wondrous activity combining as it does research, writing, preparation, props (if any), discipline, captive audience, the thrill of applause, plus the potential aftereffect in reinforcing credibility. I considered it important enough to devote a later chapter to it. This kind of persuasion can accomplish near miracles because of the psychological advantage of the speaker.

Yes, born or made, you can be a Billion Dollar Persuader and you should strive mightily toward that objective, because it means being in control of your life and getting exactly what you want out of it—money, power, fame, even love. After all, isn't getting exactly what you want out of life worth a billion dollars?

BDP Commandment 4 •	**Discover who can say yes.**
BDP Commandment 5 •	**Don't be misled by first appearances.**
BDP Commandment 6 •	**Ask great men for help regularly.**
BDP Commandment 7 •	**Protect human dignity.**
BDP Commandment 8 •	**Spend expense account money wisely and honestly.**
BDP Commandment 9 •	**Consider the emotional as well as the physical well-being of your guests when you entertain.**
BDP Commandment 10 •	**Develop a sense of humor.**
BDP Commandment 11 •	**Don't oversell or overpromote.**
BDP Commandment 12 •	**Use persuasion for good, social causes.**

★★★

4

The Exquisite Art of Communicating
★★★★★★★★★★★★★★★★★★★★★★★★★★★

Recently I stood in a doorway in a light drizzle, awaiting a friend who was to pick me up by car. There was a handsome young man near the corner, obviously waiting for someone. I assumed from his impatience that it was his girlfriend. He suddenly turned as though he had felt a presence, and sure enough, he spied his girlfriend who had turned the corner a block away. He grinned hugely and waved. She waved back, and started to walk much faster. The sound of her heels reached us then, and I could see her beaming face as she broke into a run in his direction. He moved toward her and opened his arms wide for her, still not a word having been spoken. They kissed lightly and whispered happily to each other. They had complete communication, through all the senses, plus, of course, love.

This was in contrast with what I had seen several days earlier, a catatonic withdrawal patient in a psychiatric hospital, the daughter of a friend. He, himself, appeared to be on the verge of a complete breakdown as he witnessed the severe mental illness of his child. For a variety of reasons, one being a mother who systematically destroyed her self-esteem, she had become self-destructive, believing that she was worthless and could only earn affection by doing whatever she was asked to do. Drugs, alcohol, and prostitution had practically destroyed this twenty-four-year-old girl. I went to the hospital with my friend, genuinely concerned that he might collapse or become suicidal. His daughter sat in a wheelchair facing the window of her room. Her ravaged face was immobile. Her eyes were fixed and unblinking. She neither answered nor acknowledged her grieving father's pleading words. She was totally out of communication with the rest of the human race. As muscular rigidity set in, in its inevitable course, she would die, unless—by some medical or chemical miracle—she could be restored to the living.

I begin this chapter on such a somber note because those readers who are now parents, or expect to become parents, will have nothing in life as important as preventing another person from destroying the self-esteem of a child. That is a grevious offense. There are signs of this dreadful action that should be recognized; constant criticism, ridicule, and restraint against simple childish infractions are symptoms. It would probably be better to break up a marriage than subject a child to the ravages of such a home.

There is a story about President John Kennedy that bears retelling. During a visit to the White House, his father, Joseph P. Kennedy, observed the president arriving by helicopter. Out rushed Caroline, who was crying about something. The President kissed his daughter but moved into the Oval office of the White House, saying he would be back in a moment. He did return momentarily, but later his father admonished him and told him that nothing in the world was as important as the proper attention to the needs of that child at a critical moment.

There is now general agreement that each human being is a combination of physical, intellectual, and emotional components, all interrelated.

Dr. Carl Jung has been recognized as one of the world's leading authorities on the subject. He used the term "psyche" to describe the whole human personality, a Greek word meaning spirit or soul. In modern times it has often come to mean the mind. The psyche embraces all thought, behavior, and feeling in the conscious mind. It also encompasses the *personal unconscious* and the *collective unconscious.*

In 1860 the concepts of *ego,* the center of the conscious mind, and the *personal unconscious,* as the storehouse of repressed material, were first considered and investigated. The detailed study of the *personal unconscious* was started by Sigmund Freud in 1890. Both the ego and the personal unconscious were envisioned as developing from experience.

Carl Jung took the professional world one step further. He preached that there was a third, deeper area of the psyche. He called it the *collective unconscious,* and described it as the reservoir of primordial images each person inherits from his ancestral past. According to Jung, this past includes all of a person's human ancestors, as well as his prehuman and animal ancestors. The development of the collective unconscious within human beings is not uniform. This lack of uniformity in the collective unconscious is one of the reasons people are different and unpredictable, and are never taken for granted by the Billion Dollar Persuader.

Language, and the way it is articulated, reflects the beauty and diversity of each human being. The English language is one of the greatest achievements of Western Man. Properly employed in speech and song, the human voice is a truly exquisite gift. Resolve that you will not abuse it.

A measure of the importance of man's voice was captured and immortalized by William Faulkner who said when accepting the Nobel Prize in 1950:

> It is easy enough to say that man is immortal simply because he will endure; that when the last ding-dong of doom has clanged and faded from the last worthless rock hanging tideless in the last red and dying evening that even then there will still be one more sound: that of his puny inexhaustible voice, still talking. I refuse to accept this. I believe that man will not merely endure; he will prevail. He is immortal, not because he alone among creatures has an inexhaustible voice but because he has a soul,

a spirit capable of compassion and sacrifice and endurance. The poet's, the writer's, duty is to write about these things. It is his privilege to help man endure by lifting his heart, by reminding him of the courage and honor and hope and pride and compassion and pity and sacrifice which have been the glory of his past. The poet's voice need not merely be the record of man, it can be one of the props, the pillars to help him endure and prevail.

Obviously, the first great communication with a newborn infant is touch; the second is sound, the loving sounds of a parent. There is a marvelous new development in birth procedures, originated by Dr. Frederic Leboyer, that is causing great interest. It will be a great day for the human race when it is widespread. The newborn infant is placed on the mother's stomach (if she is under sedation a doctor or nurse takes over). The infant is held and caressed with great care and tenderness. The mother croons or whispers to the infant. In the demonstrations I saw, the infant stopped crying almost immediately. And in one case, to my astonishment and joy, the infant actually seemed to smile. That kind of experience and all the other experiences of infancy, childhood and young adulthood are the first "building blocks" of the individual unconscious. The collective unconscious is more mysterious.

Biologists have advanced two views as to the development of the collective unconscious. One, known as the Lamarck theory, is that life experiences of one generation were inherited by future generations and need not be learned anew. That is, habits of one generation became the instincts of the next. It was called the Doctrine of Acquired Characteristics and is no longer considered scientifically valid. Much more popular is the evolutionary theory, which the great majority of scientists have accepted. This holds that mutations in the carrier of the genes followed the survival of the most adaptable, increasing the chances of reproduction and were passed along from generation to generation. These following specific characteristics may help to better understand the collective unconscious:

1. The brain is the primary organ of the mind, so the collective

2. Language is the primary conduit of the brain for communication.
3. The collective unconscious can be explained by acquired characteristics, mutations and natural selection, a "gift" from our human, pre-human and animal ancestors.
4. Mutations that favor adaptation, survival and reproduction are passed on. Some scientists believe we inherit predispositions from our human, pre-human and animal ancestors (for example, fear of snakes). There is controversy in social biology about this.

Be assured that this is a rare reference to biological science. It is done for a very specific purpose... to get you to improve your communication with *yourself*. Why do you want to be a Billion Dollar Persuader? For the money and the power? Or is there some force within you that tells you you should try to improve the lot of your fellow man?

There is a too often repeated tragedy in this country of ours. Men and, to an increasing degree, women get caught up in the success syndrome, reach the top in their professions and companies, and find the victories turning to ashes as they lose their spouses and children because of a lack of understanding and communication. Are you truly in communication with your inner self? If you feel that you are not, that would be a marvelous first step in becoming a Billion Dollar Persuader. You, as a human being are deep, far deeper than you may imagine. You have two reservoirs of great inner strength, your individual unconscious and your collective unconscious. But you must develop and evolve so that you can dip into these reservoirs for new energy when you feel depleted.

One of the greatest thrills in life for the truly evolved individual is the occasional communication with his collective unconscious. One of the bonuses of meditation is the message that occasionally comes from the collective unconscious. Some people call meditation "day dreaming." Dreaming in sleep seems also to connect the dreamer with his collective unconscious. De Quincy, the nineteenth-century English essayist, said of dreaming: "That facility, in alliance with the mystery of darkness, is the one great tube through which man communicates with the shadows." The personal unconscious and the collective unconscious are still such unexplored subjects that several books this size would scarcely skim the surface. What I am attempting here is a synthesis of some easy-to-comprehend aspects of this phenomenon, as a background for presenting as much as possible about the exquisite art of communicating. The principal fact, I believe, for our purposes, is the teaching of Jung that there is in the collective unconscious of every human being a prototype of an ideal to which to aspire. For the normal human being in today's world, the ideal is probably a secure, loved and respected individual who has adequate food, shelter and clothing and the resources to provide for his or her family. For the more fortunate are the added qualities of prestige, wealth, and power. As we proceed with the primary conduit from the evolved brain, talk and language, we keep uppermost in mind that those we are trying to persuade are a wonderful combination of mind, body, and emotions. And their minds are at three levels, the *conscious,* the *personal unconscious,* and the *collective unconscious,* as is yours.

We can all share and glory in the power of words, spoken or written. There are words and phrases that are awesomely powerful. One such phrase is "silent spring." It was selected as the title for a book by the late Rachel Carson. *Silent Spring* is her profoundly moving warning about the poisoning of our atmosphere and water by pollution of industry and commerce. Millions of other words had been written, but they didn't penetrate, arouse, and enrage enough people to cause the kind of action that was needed to reverse the dismal trend. She gave us the terrible vision of the day in some future spring when there would be no birds on earth. People reacted and forced their politicians to react, and for the first time positive programs were instituted to help save from extinction the birds of this country and the world.

Another kind of pollution was identified and challenged

by Newton Minnow, the chairman of the Federal Communications Commission. Once again, it was only a phrase, but it packed enormous power. He described commercial television in the United States as "that vast wasteland." The result of his creativeness was also electrifying. The public was aroused. They demanded action by their elected representatives, and the long, slow process of reversal of the dismal trend of commercial television was started. A combination of improvement of the commercial television networks and National Educational Television has given this country in 1979 an overall television system that is superb, *but ten years late.*

A long-term friend of mine, William Casey, a New York lawyer who rose to prominence in Washington, D.C., getting out of the Nixon Administration before Watergate, also created a marvelous, evocative phrase to warn the United States against a particularly dangerous type: the predatory, political prosecutors who sought to use their offices as springboards to national fame by exploiting the lamentable habit of the American press of making headlines out of charges. He called it "the Prosecutors Reign of Terror."

Another early, prescient critic of Richard M. Nixon, described what he and his administration were attempting to impose upon the United States as a "Dossier Dictatorship."

Phrasemakers may be born, but I am certain they can be made, and I advise most strongly that the aspiring persuader read everything possible, and develop an ear for the ringing, evocative, startling, shocking phrase. I have been assembling a "speech file" for a quarter of a century with at times surprising results. One phrase I adopted was used by a revivalist preacher to bemoan contemporary life. He said, from the pulpit, "Millions yearn for immortality but don't know what to do with themselves on a rainy Sunday afternoon." I used that emotional closing for a speech I was making in New Orleans. There was appreciative applause, but there was an astounding dividend minutes later. A waiter brought me a note written in a delicate, feminine hand that read, "Dear Mr. Culligan, I know what *we* could do on a rainy Sunday afternoon." I used it other times after that, but it never got the same delicious reaction.

I have dealt with touch and talk; now let us think about "the mirror of the soul"—the eyes. One of my reponsibilities as a top executive of Interpublic, the world's largest communications complex, was the perception laboratories on the top of our building on Lexington Avenue in New York. There, Interpublic supported the work of Dr. Eckhart Hess, a scientist from the University of Chicago who had become the outstanding researcher on certain aspects of animal behavior.

It was not surprising at all to Dr. Hess that the eyes of cats and dogs moved rapidly and instinctively toward items of interest. What fascinated him was that the pupils of the animals' eyes dilated and contracted according to what they were shown. So, he invented an "eye camera," which was so fast and sensitive that he could photograph the eyes of his animals and see, reflected, what they were looking at. It became simple to track the movement of the pupils and to measure the diameter of the eyes against the picture in the animals' eyes. When the pictures were developed it could be seen that two very significant things happened. The pupil of the eye would circulate around the picture with the most interesting point first, then the other elements in the picture in a kind of order of importance. The order of importance was shown by the greater or lesser dilation of the pupil. In general, things that were pleasant and good and useful caused the pupil to increase in size. Things that were dangerous or frightening caused the pupil to contract. It didn't take long to recognize that we had a breakthrough in human behavioral research. We made the first tests in our perception laboratory, showing people pictures of various subjects while photographing their eyes with a hidden camera. The results were astounding. After awhile, by simply looking at a photograph in which the eye movements were marked in sequence, and the pupil dilations or contractions were indicated, we could generally tell whether it was a man or woman. By the points of interest in a nude photo, men's eyes went one way, women's the other—young and old the same. In some cases we could tell the age of the individual. Our research became more intense and sophisticated. Ultimately we discovered that there was a difference in perception of people with blue eyes and those with brown eyes. Blue-eyed people reacted first to shape and design, secondarily to color. They tended toward pastel colors rather than bright, vivid colors. Brown-eyed people, however, reacted first to color, and secondarily to shape and design. They preferred vivid, bright colors. I recount this experience to emphasize the importance of eyes in communication and persuasion. You can learn to "read" the eyes of others. I wear a black patch over my left eye. I have a plastic device that replaces the eye lost during World War II. It really doesn't look too bad, but the tear ducts do not function normally. Tears, which flow constantly to clean and lubricate the eye, gather on the lower lid. When I became a salesman immediately after returning to civilian life I asked a very dear, old friend about the advisability of wearing a patch. He said, "Yes, by all means do. People will soon forget the patch, but without it they may spend too much time wondering which is the real eye, or why the tears are gathering. That could be a distraction and keep them from listening to what you have to say." I took his advice, and, if anything, the patch has become a useful trademark for me.

Eyes have other very unique characteristics, in addition to being the very first place a doctor looks when facing a patient. In fact, there are some diagnosticians who can make judgments about patients just by examining their eyes, either visually, or with sophisticated devices that enable the doctor to see well into the depths of the eye, including the back panel where the capillaries are. This is the only place in the human body where a doctor can get clues about the quality of the blood circulation system of the patient in direct observation, without surgery.

One characteristic of the human eye is its direct connection to the nervous system. All human beings blink their eyes regularly in order to lubricate and clean them. The normal rate of blinking is about one blink every three seconds. A person who blinks his eyes more often than that may, I say *may*, be under stress. If, in addition to the rapid eye blink rate, there is a dampness and coldness to their hands, you can be quite sure the individual is under unusual stress, if not physically ill.

So, before you meet a new prospect for the first time, you would do well to check your own eye blink rate, and the condition of your hands. You may be showing signs of stress that may be evident to the possible client. There are simple exercises which can be easily learned to manage the stresses which are a part of life. If you walk into a prospect's office and see a too-rapid eye blink rate, and if his hands are cold and damp, you would be wise to do something to reduce the stress before you start the serious business of selling. There are many little diversions which suggest themselves in the average office, pictures, trophies, awards, artwork, books, etc.

Touching, talking, seeing... how about hearing and smelling? The aspiring persuader must know how to use his ears... to *listen*. The human voice can be an indicator of stress. I can actually tell that some people are under stress by the sound of their voices. I do not mean stuttering, which can be far more than nervousness or stress. (A parenthetical note about stuttering. If you do stutter there is a strong possibility that you became mad as hell about somebody or something when you were a child. Therapy has been most effective in the alleviation of this cruel problem. It takes time, but it is well worth the investment.)

The voice is a combination of AM and FM sound waves. Stress can cause diminution or elimination of FM, causing the voice to sound harsh and reedy. I found this out when president of NBC Radio. I noticed that my voice sounded different at times, particularly when I was overworked, but also if I got a call from General Sarnoff about some problem. I had a sound engineer record my voice during relaxed times, and I had him install a recorder in my office that I could activate. We compared the sound of my voice and sure enough, found that the FM sound waves disappeared during heavy stress, giving my voice a strained, unnatural sound. So, the persuader listens to the opening remarks of the new prospect. If his voice sounds unnatural, the persuader should try to reduce the stress in some amiable way.

As for the sense of smell, there are fewer opportunities to use this sense, but they do exist. At one point in my early days of part-time work I was a canvasser. My job was to start at the top of each office building and stop in at every office, ask for the office manager and offer a free demonstration of an office machine. If that was refused, I was to leave a brochure describing the quality of the product. There were many secretaries who would not cooperate in getting me to the office manager, and a few would call the building superintendent and complain that "peddlers were in the building." A friend once gave me a tip that increased my success many times over. He sent me to one of the small perfume companies in my territory where I was able to buy a large number of small bottles of perfume at a very low rate. I tied my card to the bottles and handed them out to the secretaries. I did get to see more office managers, and only rarely did a building superintendent chase me out of a building. The persuader should keep in mind that flowers and perfume have their uses, though now of course many of the secretaries are men and the superintendents women.

That leaves only the "sixth sense," and now we have come full circle, back to the starting point, the entire human being, the marvelous combination of mind, body, and emotions. Back to the psyche, the combination of the conscious mind, the personal unconscious and the collective unconscious. It is in the latter two levels of the human psyche that the "sixth sense" lives. That is where the survival instinct is centered. I say with the firmest conviction that the true Billion Dollar Persuader, either by design or good fortune, has a quality of honesty and dependability about him or her that appeals to the "sixth sense" of the prospects and to their instinct to survive and prosper.

There will, unfortunately, always be conmen and conwomen, finding marks to swindle. Most of the marks will be easy prey because they themselves are not entirely honest or are looking for something for nothing. But the persuader must have a basic honesty and integrity to start with. As he and she matures, credibility grows. These qualities mold the look of the persuader. They show in the eyes, the smile, the posture, the voice. They appeal to the sixth sense of the prospect, the yearning for survival, security and prosperity. Few have said it better than Shakespeare:

> This above all: to thine own self be true,
> And it must follow, as the night the day,
> Thou canst not then be false to any man.

In the broadest possible sense there are two distinct kinds of persuasion, which I will examine in the next two chapters. The most interesting and, at times, noble kind is concept persuasion, the selling of great ideas, otherwise known as intangibles. The second kind I call product persuasion, though it will include services of a specific nature.

BDP Commandment 13 • **Look at all human beings as physical, intellectual, and emotional combinations.**

BDP Commandment 14 • **Remember your reservoirs of inner strength: your individual and collective unconscious.**

BDP Commandment 15 • **Develop your own phrase-making ability, if possible, or borrow from others.**

BDP Commandment 16 • **Start and build a "Speech File."**

BDP Commandment 17 • **Learn to read the signs of stress in yourself and others: excessive eye blink rate, cold, moist hands, "reedy" voice.**

BDP Commandment 18 • **Avoid or correct facial distractions and gestures.**

BDP Commandment 19 • **Listen.**

★★★

5

Concept Persuasion

★★★★★★★★★★★★★★★★★★★★★★★★★★★★

There is an ingredient in the psyche that gives some men and women the ability to sell concepts. Not all people can. In a word, this ingredient is *overview*, the ability to see and understand the interrelationships of things that are important in themselves. In past times this was called seeing "the big picture." Obviously, most people would want to be able to see and understand the overall picture, but in forty years of all kinds of social, military, and business situations, I have met very few leaders and executives who really do have overview. Some think they do and do not. They are possibly the most dangerous.

Perhaps the quickest way for me to describe what I mean by interrelationships is to think in terms of energy. It takes energy to get anything done. A man expends a certain amount of energy in his activities. A woman does, too. When they interrelate and marry, a new dynamic is created because of the miracle of nature. They create something together they could not create alone: a baby. That is the simplest but most profound interrelationship in this world of ours. Then let us say this man, woman, and child live in a neighborhood next to another man, woman, and child. Each home has its own combined energy of the three members of each family. Suppose they decided to combine energies in building a swimming pool together that they couldn't afford to build separately. They create a new dynamic in that interrelationship. Let us look for a moment at something much more complex.

The United States has these major problems, all crying out for solution:

Unemployment
Inadequate transportation, road and rail
Ecology—environmental problems
Rural poverty
Urban blight
Dependance on foreign oil
Indigent old and dependent young.

Each of these problems resists solution because of the enormous amount of time and energy necessary plus the huge dollar investments required for rapid solutions. But some of these problems could be solved better and quicker and cheaper if they were interrelated. For example, I devised a program that I called Relatus, which involved the simultaneous solution of problems in which the same people and equipment could be used in an interrelated program. That is, the trucks used for the building of roads could be used to remove industrial wastes from nearby cities and the waste could be buried under the new roads. Trees and bushes could be planted in an organized program using the same trucks, equipment, and some of the men employed in the road building. I hope someday to convince a state of the federal government to accept Relatus as a method of solving problems more quickly, more humanely, and more cheaply in interrelationships instead of individually.

Admittedly, the title of this book is grandiose, but in this chapter will be described some examples of persuasion that are not overwhelmed by the billion dollar designation. The prime example is The European Common Market. The Common

Market was the concept of Jean Monnet, a Frenchman from rural France, who specifically remembered when the idea first dawned on his nine-year-old mind.

Mr. Monnet, Sr., was a vintner in a French village in which there was constant unrest and friction between the property owners, the workers, some of whom were Communists, and the Roman Catholic Church. Young Jean Monnet became aware of the life around his family at about age five. He "felt" the tension and was confused by it. One day his father told him to rush to the monsignor of the church and request that he ring the church bells as a frost warning, a recurring threat to the vineyards, the village's principal source of employment and income. Jean Monnet followed those instructions and those that followed in rapid order as the entire village mobilized to protect the vineyards. Some of the measures were most severe. Many of the older men actually protected the youngest, most vulnerable vines with their bodies. They slept in the nurseries using their body warmth to keep the tender vines alive. Others worked tirelessly to wrap vines in burlap and to light smudge pots that provided warmth. The crop was saved, and within hours the old conflicts resumed. Jean Monnet remembers asking his father, "Why don't people help each other *all* the time?" His father's answer was a shrug.

As Jean Monnet matured and learned of the death, devestation, and suffering of the French and other Europeans in the countless, reoccurring wars throughout history on that tortured continent, the idea of the Common Market gradually emerged. It didn't become a reality for four decades, but when it did, a new age for humanity in Europe began. The best single evidence of the brilliance of Jean Monnet and the validity of his concept is that it would be virtually impossible to find a sane person in Europe who would believe that a war between Western European countries is any longer possible.

In our own country, Franklin Delano Roosevelt was our "concept persuader," in the political arena, with his conception of the New Deal and in the human area with his concept about the elimination of polio, the age-old scourge from which the president himself suffered.

In contrast, a concept that did not succeed in persuading a sufficient number of Americans to espouse it was the beautiful dream of Albert Schweitzer, summed up in his phrase, reverence for life. What a totally different world this would be if that concept had been as persuasive as the ideas for the European Common Market, the New Deal, and eliminating polio. The solutions to most of the world's problems can be found in true reverence for life. At its core would be the solution to the problems of poverty and overpopulation. If all adults had a true reverence for life, no parents would have more children than they could adequately take care of. Crimes of violence, recklessness on the highways, rape, battering of children and wives would be nonexistent rather than extensive and growing. Why did Albert Schweitzer fail during the same general period in which Jean Monnet and Franklin D. Roosevelt succeeded? Albert Schweitzer was a "loner," lived in faraway Africa, was not a highly visible personality, and had no "power base." He appealed only to the conscience of the humanitarians of the world during a time when there were other terrible forces at work. There is room for doubt that Jean Monnet could have gained acceptance in Europe for the Common Market without the help of Schumann, a brilliant French politician who orchestrated the selling of the Common Market.

Consider the uneven record of another president, John Fitzgerald Kennedy. How can we account for the fact that he inspired the people and the Congress of the United States to get to the moon within a decade, at a cost of billions of dollars and trillions of man-hours, but was unable to get the Congress to pass his legislative program for the country during his all too brief presidency? It was only after his assassination that the awesomely effective Lyndon Baines Johnson was able to persuade the Congress to pass the same Kennedy program. Some experts believe that President Kennedy dissipated some of his power by the Bay of Pigs fiasco, and alienated the business leadership of the country. He was quoted as saying "all businessmen are sons of bitches." What he actually did say was that his father had told him that all businessmen are sons of bitches. There is a profound lesson in this enormous contrast between the Kennedy who could and did inspire his countrymen to make the sacrifices necessary to catch up and outdistance our principal world enemy, the Soviet Union, in the race to outer space, and the Kennedy who could not move the Congress to pass his legislative program. Through his own errors and those of this administration he dissipated the good will of the Congress.

Two Billion Dollar Persuaders lived less than forty miles apart, but, politically might well have been on different planets. One was Winston Churchill, the leader who persuaded France to fight on after occupation by the Nazis, and Patrick Pearse, the leader-orator-poet of the Easter Rebellion in Ireland in 1916.

It was the night France had surrendered to the Germans. Storm troopers had paraded down the Champs Elysées, and the spirit of that great country was flickering out. Winston Churchill went on the air that night with this message to the French people:

> Good night then, and sleep. Sleep to gather strength for the dawn. For the dawn will surely come, brightly will it shine on the brave and true and those who suffer for a good cause, and gloriously on the tombs of heroes.

To this day—four decades later—those words still move me close to tears. The French did gather strength for the dawn, both in France and in exile around the world. Imagine its effect on the millions of French men and women to whom it was the only voice of faith and hope. It was, to be sure, an emotional appeal, but one common characteristic of the world's greatest persuaders has been their willingness and their ability to be emotional without mawkishness when the need was great. The least emotional leader in modern times was probably Charles de Gaulle. But when he let roll out his rallying cry, the Glory of France, there was little need for emotionalism on *his* part. His audiences supplied all the emotionalism necessary.

Churchill and de Gaulle spoke from positions of great power and prestige. Not so Patrick Pearse, leader of a ragtag band of revolutionaries. He spoke for a race that had lost every rebellion for three hundred years, averaging one every fifty years. Pearse became a Billion Dollar Persuader purely on the strength of his thoughts and words:

> Life springs from death, and from the graves of patriotic men and women spring living nations. The Defenders of this Realm have worked well in secret and in the open. They think that they have pacified Ireland. They think that they have purchased half of us and intimidated the other half. They think that they have foreseen everything, think that they have provided against everything; but the fools, the fools, the fools! They have left us our Fenian dead, and while Ireland holds these graves, Ireland unfree shall never be at peace.

These flaming words ignited patriotic time bombs all over Ireland. They, and other inspirational words led to the "Glorious Folly" of the 1916 Easter Rebellion. Six years later the Republic of Ireland became a reality.

Those are examples of concept persuasion on a grand scale, a scale beyond the scope of all but that handful of men at the right place at the right time for heroic words and deeds. Here are some examples of concept persuasion on a much more practical scale.

Alexander Shields had a flair as a young man for design of men's and women's clothes. He also had a concept that was quite original for its time. He embraced the view that "less is more." It led him to understatement in his clothes. He didn't believe that clothes should just be comfortable. He believed that extreme good looks and attractiveness should be sought after and worked on. He had awesome competition, being on Park Avenue at 58th Street, in New York City, surrounded by the most intense and often jealous adversaries for affluent and style conscious customers. Alexander Shields has been in the same location, still espousing that "less is more" philosophy for thirty years He later said, "lesser is better," and finally, "the least is best." His clothes, his shop, his people are a delight, for his concept is one of increasing simplicity.

New Yorkers like to think of their city as the Big Apple. There is a place in Chicago that many people think of as "the bowl of apples." This place is the reception room of the Leo Burnett Advertising Agency. In 1935 a charming concept led to a lovely and probably healthy tradition. A young advertising man named Leo Burnett with seven associates decided to open an advertising agency. It was the depths of the depression. There were derisive hoots about that decision, and when the bowl of apples appeared with the invitation to all visitors to help themselves, a newspaper columnist said, "It won't be long 'till Leo Burnett is selling apples on the street corner instead of giving them away." Well, for quite a few years Leo Burnett has been giving away over 200,000 apples a year in its United States offices alone. To Leo Burnett and his friends the red apple was a symbol of warmth and Midwestern hospitality, as well as a kind of personal statement to the business world: "We're nice, normal folks, and we know how to reach all those other nice normal folks through good advertising."

A man in Atlanta had a concept that everywhere in America men, women, and children ought to be able to get a tasty, soft drink that was always of the same purity and taste. But he didn't want to be shipping water all over the country, so he decided to ship syrup all over the country, and also demand that the same kind of good soda water be used locally. That became the basis for the Coca-Cola Company. Then a man arrived one day with a two-word idea that changed the nature of the company. He said "bottle it." For decades the concept of Coca-Cola was "the best cola drink for a nickle." When the economics changed, and the price could no longer be continued, the concept changed from the cola business to the "refreshment business" and today Coca-Cola sells orange juice and a wide range of other soft drinks in bottles. Incidentally, I met a doctor in Atlanta whose wife had a somewhat different concept about what to do with two hundred thousand dollars the couple had to invest. His concept was to put it into Coca-Cola stock. Her concept was to build a new house. As so often happens, or haven't you noticed, the lady's concept reigned supreme. That two hundred thousand dollars would be worth twenty million now. Wonder how he felt every time he looked at the house... and his wife?

Regrettably, there are concepts that are valid which could, even should succeed, which do not because of conditions beyond the control of the originator. I thought, for example, that the Auto Train concept was a natural, given the oil shortage, the convenience factors, and the safety considerations of very long drives across country. One simply drove the family car to the railroad station, watched it stored safely aboard, and then enjoyed the comfort of the train ride a thousand miles or more. A substantial business was developed. However, ageing equipment and less-than-adequate roadbeds caused two derailments. The losses were enormous. There is still a very good possibility that Auto Train will be a success, but there have been headaches and heartaches galore for the founders and managers of this company. There is a good lesson involved here. If you have a choice, and there are times the concept persuader may not, try to operate in an area in which there is as much control of the important factors as possible.

Rutledge Bermingham, a young businessman, noticed that even though the services and equipment of a railroad he used regularly were running down, the water in the cooler was about the best he had ever tasted. He made enquiries and found that the railroad owned the land in the foothills of the mountains in which the clear spring was located that served the railroad with its water. The general area was known as Deer Park. He acquired the rights to use the spring and founded a bottled water company that has become very successful. He sold out his interest to the Nestlé Company. The bottled water industry in the United States is burgeoning, given the conditions of pollution, waste, and taste. Bermingham was among the pioneers. Unfortunately, as so often has happened, the "pioneers get killed by the Indians." He made the error of believing that he would continue to run his business within Nestlé. Rarely does that concept work. He was eased out within two years. Gigantic corporations do not like individualists.

The cosmetics business is largely built on concepts and promotion. As this book is being readied for production I am having the great pleasure of participating in a promotion concept of Ultima II, a division of Revlon. Several years ago Ultima decided to try to increase the traffic in the cosmetic departments by having a storewide presence. They accomplished this by a concept involving displays that were totally in harmony with their products. As the luck of the Irish would have it, the Spring 1979 promotion is "The Colors of Ireland" and is the inspiration for various other departments of the store. The "Colors of Ireland" promotion was featured in some windows, and in locations throughout the store, using exquisite pictures shot in Ireland and featuring one of the most famous models in America, Lauren Hutton. I was invited to participate because I had written a book about Ireland, and the book jacket phased in beautifully with Ultima's "Colors of Ireland." The fashion and cosmetics industries are marvelous training grounds and careers for people with a flair.

For some years I was privileged to know and work for an extraordinary concept persuader: General David Sarnoff. My direct contacts with him were infrequent, but I read all his speeches avidly.

My first meeting with the General was a shocker. It was at the entrance to the ballroom of the Waldorf-Astoria Hotel on opening day of the NBC affiliates meeting, the first I had ever attended. While moving slowly toward the entrance I spied David Adams, the brightest and one of the nicest of the old-line NBC executives. I called out, "David, David." He didn't hear me, but another David did. David Sarnoff turned around, grabbed my hand and said "Welcome, glad to see you." I thought, *Thank God he thought I was an affiliate.* Calling General Sarnoff "David" was beyond me, even after nine years at NBC.

David Sarnoff was born in 1891 in Minsk, in Russia. He had great natural intelligence but little formal education, an iron constitution, driving ambition, and a knack for very effective personal communication. He entered the electronics field as a radio technician, broadcasting through the establishment of a patent pool by the leading electronics companies. Little did they suspect that the tiny company they started would grow to challenge them in their own fields and become paramount in broadcasting. But David Sarnoff *knew*.

Basically, the Radio Corporation of America was a radio equipment license holder, owned by AT&T, General Electric, and Westinghouse. Later, broadcasting became a sideline and a promotional force to get the public to buy radios and encourage businessmen to put advertising revenues into the burgeoning medium. Local radio stations were the principal customers for the products manufactured by RCA.

Radio networking was the next logical step. With its development side by side with air transport, the United States started to become one community. The effects of extensive travel opportunities and instant communications via telephone and network radio were profound and unparalleled. In some miraclous way Sarnoff envisioned this very early. Sectional and regional differences flattened out and a national style appeared. Speech patterns changed, humor changed, and for the first time in American history, a statement like "Wanna buy a duck?" the punch line of the old comic Joe Penner, would get the same hilarious response in any of the forty-eight states. Television and the jet completed the trend. The United States, vast, complicated, still growing and changing (particularly because of the move of its minorities) did become one community. The National Broadcasting Company tied it together.

David Sarnoff had that combination rarely seen: prescience of vision and practicality. Linking together radio stations into a loose confederation was Sarnoff's next huge contribution to RCA, the United States, and the world. How long the idea was in process is not known, but the radio network concept was outlined in 1926. The major aim was to create a greater demand for sets by better service to the public. To develop this business, Sarnoff formed the National Broadcasting Company. RCA and

NBC were now on a path to a great, new profitable industry, radio networking, but by no means exclusively. Three years *before* forming NBC as a radio network, Sarnoff, in April 1923, said, "I believe television will come to pass in due course." Not many agreed with him at that time. Most did, however, sixteen years later when RCA-NBC gave the public its first full demonstration of black and white television. In a spine-tingling presentation, Sarnoff almost religiously intoned, "Now at last we add sight to sound."

The diversity of his excellent mind astonished many. For while he was providing motive power to television, he was also stimulating thought and research. Some of his statements had a missionary zeal—"The mystery of the atom, including its nuclear physics and the curious isotopes tracing unlimited frontiers, beckons youth just as the telegraph key enchanted the newsboy, Edison." He was always talking, talking…teaching and persuading.

In 1946, when army scientists made radar contact with the moon, Sarnoff said:

> The radar signal from the moon proved that man might some day reach out to touch the planets; it revived speculation on interplanetary communication, and inspired great hope for interstellar exploration.…He may even learn how to use the moon and the planets as radio soundboards and reflectors to bounce or relay broadcasts and to mirror television pictures.

David Sarnoff was an inspirational speaker on any subject. Of individual enterprise he said:

> The chase for security is elusive, like the chase for happiness. The Eskimo has security, but how much progress has he made? Progress isn't measured by security. Too often a fellow who wants security wants to occupy a $5,000 a year job with a $50,000 a year income. I don't think money itself represents security. The person who has ability to earn a living has far greater security than the person who merely has money. Personally, I prefer a life of adventure to a life of security.

Sarnoff religiously believed that the essence of leadership was to make people "perform" better as a team than they thought they could. In 1951, on Sarnoff's forty-fifth anniversary in radio, the RCA laboratories in Princeton, N.J., was renamed the David Sarnoff Research Center. It is now accepted as one of the finest research facilities of its kind in the world. There was a very special anniversary celebration on this occasion and Sarnoff, instead of simply accepting the gift, challenged the staff to make the renaming of the center meaningful by delivering to him, in five years, three new developments. He asked for an electronic amplifier of light; a magnetic tape recorder for black and white and color television; and an electronic air conditioner. When, on September 30, 1956, the RCA labs did deliver these "gifts," he said: "A few of the scientists and research men who heard me make these specific challenges to their ingenuity wondered if I quite grasped the toughness of the problems involved. If I did, they said, I might not have had the gall to set a five-year limit for their solution. But I have often had more faith in these men than they had in themselves. I had no doubts that they could solve these problems, and I even thanked them in advance for the presents I confidently expected to receive tonight."

During the spring of 1978 President Jimmy Carter gave a birthday party at the White House. The party was for Bob Hope, my personal favorite persuader in entertainment. This true story, told to me by the late Jimmy Saphier, one of Bob Hope's agents, will tell volumes about this delightful and incomparable man.

One day Bob Hope dropped into the office of Saphier and casually dropped a legal-looking document on his desk. Jimmy picked it up, looked in amazement at a certificate establishing him as ten percent owner of TV station KOA in Denver, Colorado. He asked Bob Hope, "What's this?" and Hope replied "You're my ten percenter, aren't you?" and left Jimmy Saphier practically in tears. Years later, when the TV station was sold for over $7 million Jimmy Saphier's ten percent was worth

$700,000 on a capital gain basis.

Along with his innate comic ability, Hope has a super endowment of wit, intelligence, a prodigious memory (he believes he has about a quarter of a million jokes somewhere in his memory bank), an iron constitution, a remarkable talent for introspection and self-evaluation, and oversized feelings for others, particularly toward those who most needed what he had to give: the men in military service all around the world. By 1961, Bob Hope had given up eighteen Christmases at home to be with American servicemen in some of the globe's most remote places. In that year, Senator Stuart Symington introduced a resolution to Congress calling Bob Hope "America's most prized ambassador of good will in the world."

Gales of laughter followed him wherever he showed his puckish face. He ripped off lines like, "Were the boys in the last camp glad to see me! They actually got down on their knees—what a spectacle—what a tribute—what a crap game."

Next to comedy, Hope loves golf, and he has been and still is very good at it. He is capable of a golf score in the low 70s. He admits to losing his cool only once in competitive golf, when he was teamed with President Eisenhower. As he describes it, "We were teamed in a tournament and I went to pieces and shot an eighty-three—we lost." Hope went on, "The next day I played against him, this time for money, and shot a seventy-three. As he paid me off he ribbed, "Why didn't you play like that yesterday?"

The superiority of Sylvester L. (Pat) Weaver is now incontrovertibly in the record. He was the Program Director of NBC Television and then its president. Nothing can dim the luster of his contributions to television: "Today" and "Tonight," "Your Show of Shows," "Wide Wide World," "The Comedy Hour," the Hallmark Hall of Fame, all part of the Weaver Programming concept.

Weaver also made another very valuable contribution in his conceptualization of the marketing aspects of broadcasting. His vision, his daring and his originality placed him solidly in that small group of individuals who are said to be ahead of their time.

He was, as an admiring wag put it, the only man who could reminisce about the future. A few examples will clearly demonstrate the truth of his assertion.

The television special or spectacular was a Weaver creation. The idea was to break the normal programming habit regularly, to preempt regular shows to present to America the unusual, the occasionally uplifting. But the first time Pat Weaver did it was in radio, in 1933. He was the first man in America to buy one entire day's programming on a national radio network to introduce a new product. When he moved into television he brought the idea along, adapted for this very different medium. Soon all three networks were doing specials.

Weaver joined NBC-TV as Director of Programming in 1949; he came from one of the giants of the advertising business, the Young and Rubicam agency, where he had been in charge of "The Fred Allen Show" on NBC radio. Although Pat brought ideas from radio and some radio-oriented personnel with him, he very quickly became sensitive to the power, promise, and potential of television. In October 1950, *Variety* reported on "Pat Weaver's Dramatic Plan:" made-for-TV movies and the telecasting of legitimate theater from Broadway. "Weaver put considerable stress on the need to 'exercise an attitude of humility and a sense of mission in dealing with television,' asserting that NBC's blueprint calls for the development of TV 'as a medium of real mass interest for outdistancing any other known medium.'"

In August 1951, Weaver described global television as a certainty. It could take time, he conceded, but it would come, and he began immediately to lay the foundations. There were only sixteen million sets in the U.S. around this time, a few million in Great Britain, and in countries like Canada, Japan, Russia, West Germany, Italy, and France, television was only just on the verge of being born. Nevertheless, new and strange-sounding names ranged through the halls of NBC: Emilio Azcarrago of Mexico, Fernando Eileta of Panama, and Goar Mestre of Havana. These men, along with CBC representatives from Montreal and Toronto, were to bring their authority, ownership, and considerable power to bear in establishing an alliance with NBC.

One of the greatest problems facing broadcasting at this time, in both radio and television, was the way it was financed. To put it bluntly, the industry was a slave to the advertisers and, to an even greater extent, the advertising agencies. All the networks did was rent their facilities and sell airtime to the agencies for the sponsors. The agencies, therefore, controlled most of the programming: they put the shows together, hired the performers, and staged the programs. The sales forces at the networks were really only *service* forces who mainly dealt with the broadcasting experts at the agencies; the agency men sold the ideas to the bill-paying sponsors. The so-called salesmen from the networks "serviced the agencies" and rarely ever dealt with the sponsors's advertising directors.

One result of this was the identification of programs with the sponsoring company: "Texaco Star Theatre," "Ford Television Theatre," "Kraft Theatre," "Philco Television Theatre," "Colgate Comedy Hour," "General Electric Theatre," "Alcoa Playhouse," "Camel News Caravan," "Gillette Cavalcade of Sports," "The Voice of Firestone," and many others. Another result, however, was the tendency toward bland programming, for the agencies would seldom dare to risk the sponsor's money—and their own commissions.

This lack of adventure, of creativity, of risk-taking is, of course, a matter of dollars. The sponsor of a show wants a formula that will guarantee him the greatest possible audience at the least possible cost. And that formula was worked out by Paul Klein, a former Director of Audience Research at NBC, as the Theory of the Least Objectionable Program. That is, as Martin Mayer, critic and author, says, "Since people are going to watch television anyway, the show which the fewest people find unpleasant will get the biggest rating." Revolting? Yes! But that was the way it was.

Coming from an advertising agency himself and being the kind of person he is, Weaver was acutely aware of this situation. Speaking of that time, he has said, "I brought in some of the top ad agency programming men to help me at NBC and I told them, 'Look, we ruined radio. Let's not let it happen to television. Let's stage our own programs and just sell advertising time to the agencies.'" His plan, however, involved more than just wresting control of programming away from the sponsors and the agencies; it was also a blueprint for considerably expanding the spectrum of television programs. Pat's brainchild was called the "magazine concept" and it required both a new philosophy of programming and a new approach to sales.

Briefly, Pat conceived of a week's television as being like a well-stocked newstand, something for everyone. There would certainly still be the mass-audience programs, especially in prime time when Daddy was home and all-family viewing swelled the ratings. The economics of television demanded that. But, Pat insisted, there was also an audience for limited-interest programs—just as there was a market for special-interest magazines. He wanted shows for brilliant talk, drama, ballet, sports, and commentary to be scattered over the daytime, latenight, and weekend time slots.

And just as an advertiser could buy space in a magazine or in a series of magazines—in order to reach his potential customers or to maintain public awareness of his company—so would he have the opportunity to buy sixty seconds or thirty seconds or even a shorter time at various times of the day to do the same thing. In both cases, the advertiser has no control over the contents of the other pages in the magazine or the other blocks of time in the schedule. The advertiser would thus be taking fewer risks with his investment, since a low rating in one time would be balanced by a high rating in another. But more importantly, the creation of programs would not be based solely on commercial considerations.

Weaver began the transition to the new approaches required by the magazine concept on two fronts. Fortunately, he could count on his own uncanny ability to select exactly the right person to do a job. First, he created the Program-Sales Department at NBC, and he made Mike Dann (who was later to rise to the top of the CBS program department) its first manager.

Mike's function was to bridge the gap between programming and sales. This was essential because it would be necessary when whole one-hour and half-hour shows could be bought by the top ten advertising agencies in New York and Chicago acting for their clients.

Second, Pat conceived the outrageous notion of a magazine format television show to be broadcast from seven to nine each weekday morning. If it had not been for his extraordinary position at NBC at the time, both the idea and the man would have been laughed out of the building. Pat persisted, however, and forced the experiment at great expense and considerable risk.

The question of who could bind such a show together was an extremely knotty one. People would be only half-awake and would range in mood from uncivil to grouchy. Loud noises and boffo humor were out of the question. Since there would be much talk, the star would need to have the knack of good-humored, low-key interviewing. There would be some muted entertainment and news—*lots* of news and features. Pat came up with exactly the right choice: the mild, shy, highly intelligent, and creative Dave Garroway. Garroway fit the "Today" format: he was tactful, gentle, and extraordinarily well-read. He had a computerlike memory and an inquisitive mind. His vocal and visual signature—the raised hand with the palm facing outward and the single word, "Peace," delivered almost prayerfully— was also exactly right. Pat Weaver married concept and talent, and the marriage worked. In time "The Today Show" will gross a billion dollars. Now in its twenty-sixth year it represents the greatest single concept persuasion in all of broadcasting.

I have been amused over the years as others have taken the credit for the incredible success of "The Today Show." One great creative man of "Today" who did not forget my contributions was Gerald Green, who was one of my particular favorites on the "Today" staff. Gerald Green went on to become one of America's most popular authors (*The Last Angry Man, His Majesty O'Keefe, The Pitiless Light*) but his finest contribution was the shocking reminder of the Nazi brutality in his brilliantly written *Holocaust.*

Gerald Green is a Billion Dollar Persuader of a quite different type. He accomplished a feat during 1978 and 1979 which is monumental. The horror of Nazism has been portrayed for decades in various techniques. There have been books, magazine articles, lecturer, theatrical motion pictures, live television appearances and radio programs. Each was effective in some way, but they tended to further convince people who were already convinced and leave the majority of non-Jews unmoved. Then Gerald Green wrote *Holocaust.* It exploded on the consciousness of American non-Jews and made the first really deep impression. There was resistance to *Holocaust,* some of it from leading Jews. There was criticism from many sources. There was a possibility that *Holocaust* might not be shown elsewhere in the world, particularly in those countries needing it the most, Germany, England, Italy and Japan. But the breakthrough happened and *Holocaust* reached a very high percentage of the German people, particularly the young. The effect has been, and will continue to be, profound.

I was one of the "youngsters" picked out of obscurity by Pat Weaver, and given the opportunities that permitted me to become a Billion Dollar Persuader. Pat was an inspiration to me, and I watched and studied his every move. One of the keys to his success was his facility for overview. He could step back from everyday problems and see interrelationships and changing forces that had to lead to change. I know he believed that he could lead the change rather than be the victim or "passenger" of that change. I determined to emulate Pat Weaver in that overview capability. Two of the concepts that resulted were NBC "News on the Hour" and imagery transfer, mentioned previously.

Jo Ransom told the advertising world about imagery transfer in the usual breezy manner of *Variety,* the bible of show business. It was Robert Lewis Shayon who institutionalized imagery transfer in the highly prestigous *Saturday Review.* Under the head "Beware of I.T." he wrote:

Do your feelings bother you when you listen to radio commercials? Mood Master commercials will take charge of them when the new broadcasting season begins, according to Matthew J. Culligan....Mr. Culligan has this to say about "evocative commercials:"Just as radio programming will synthesize sound to build extra values, so too will the "imagery transfer" advertiser take advantage of the way the human mind works. Use of mood-creating devices will be an integral part of his commercials .... "Simply put," he states, "imagery transfer stresses the creative use of psychological findings. It involves the conscious production of emotional effects through the careful employment of musical and linguistic sounds as sound."

When this kind of publicity had penetrated the business community as well as the advertising fraternity I carefully selected my first targets for imagery transfer sales. Here again I remembered the lessons learned with NBC News on the Hour, a previous personal triumph. When I looked with dismay on the ratings of fifteen-minute shows three times a day, I cringed. Television was delivering much larger audiences. The highest level support was necessary for any change in the old format, in which a few favored advertisers got all the benefits of the three-quarter-hour news programs. Also, the affiliates had all the rest of the most desirable times of the morning and evening. I first had to persuade my management that a format change was absolutely necessary. I did it by an outrageously emotional appeal to Robert Sarnoff and other members of the NBC executive council:

Gentlemen, the proud old NBC Radio Network is dying. It needs major surgery, *now*. If the surgery is not performed now the NBC Radio Network will die by inches. The surgery is not guaranteed to succeed, but shouldn't it be tried, and if it must, let the patient die with dignity.

I was permitted to change the format of NBC Radio, putting "News on the Hour" on *seventeen* times a day in five-minute hunks rather than three times a day in fifteen-minute portions. This permitted the spread of shorter commercials over many hours of the day with the automatic doubling and tripling of the ratings, with no increase in cost. But what to do with this bonanza? The old way would have been to take in a dozen or several dozen more advertisers, with the increased costs of more salesmen and more sales servicemen, more merchandising costs, more headaches. I decided on a bold stroke: sell the entire package of "News on the Hour" to one sponsor. My associates were aghast; that package cost $4 million a year. *That* was a television-sized budget. No advertiser in his right mind would risk that kind of money on radio, they said. I compromised, and set the policy that two advertisers would share "News on the Hour" at $2.2 million each. And by God, we did. The Bristol-Myers Company, and Brown and Williamson Tobacco Company signed contracts, and the NBC Radio Network was on its way back to profitability.

With the lesson of "News on the Hour" very much in mind, I set the policy for the sale of imagery transfer. The whole idea was based on the ability to trigger mental images and bring them then into focus by key words of the original experience as seen on television or in magazines. If there was validity to the argument, then the trigger mechanism could be brief, as long as expertly done. I adopted the policy of fifteen-second commercials only, scattering them throughout seventeen hours of programming, again taking advantage of the dispersion to accumulate greater and greater audiences. NBC sold $4 million in fifteen-second commercials during the first year.

Still another great persuader in my life was John Kingsley Herbert, who was also at NBC as Executive Vice President in Charge of Sales. We met first when he was sales manager of *Good Housekeeping*. As part of the audience for a presentation from the advertising agency for *Good Housekeeping*, I learned another unforgettable lesson. The advertising agency came roaring in with a recommendation that *Good Housekeeping Magazine* make a motion picture at a cost of some twenty thousand dollars. Herbert listened courteously, and ended the meeting with the statement, "Absolutely not, if our product, *Good Housekeeping Magazine*, is so good, why do we need a motion picture to sell it?"

In April 1955 I was permitted to form a new division that I called Telesales over the opposition of the NBC lawyers who were terrified of any expansion because of the gimlet eyes of the Department of Justice and the Federal Communications Commission. I said simply, "Let's do it, make it profitable; then if we are attacked, let's sell Telesales for a nice profit. In the meantime we'll sell millions of dollars worth of television." I wanted to sell television shows by using closed circuit television directly into clients' offices or hotel conference rooms where prospects could be assembled. Shortly after the announcement George Rosen of *Variety* wrote:

PAT AND BOB—TV BOY ACTORS
SELLING SHOWS GLAMOROUS WAY

The era of electronic salesmanship has achieved full-blown status at NBC-TV. What actually is going on these days, little-known except to those close to the scene of operations, is a whole new phase of show business into which is being poured as much energy, resourcefulness, and administrative acumen (not to mention coin) as some of the networks major TV attractions.

It all goes under the heading of Telesales. It has one object—to convince the advertiser to buy NBC television shows. On a practically day-by-day basis, the high administrative command, topped by Prexy Pat Weaver and Exveep Bob Sarnoff, stand by awaiting a call from Joe Culligan, manager of sales (and in this case doubling as casting director) to don makeup and go on a special closed circuit or film presentation.

One particular Telesale was a sheer delight to Pat Weaver and me, and a source of consternation and jealousy to the competition. Pat wanted some worthwhile programming on Sunday, to counter the image of that day as the intellectual ghetto. He told me to take dead aim at the Hallmark Greeting Card Company for sponsorship of a dramatic show that he wanted to call "The Hall of Fame." "Hallmark Hall of Fame" had a nice ring to it, so I jumped at the opportunity. I spent many hours on the research and planning for the presentation, so it would be consistent with the tone and quality of the fine dramatic shows Pat Weaver felt he had to have. I decided on a technique that succeeded beyond my fondest hopes. Maurice Evans had done "Hamlet" for television, and a film of it was available. I screened it several times and found one sequence in which Evans, alone and at his very best, did a monologue. I supplemented it and used the result in the presentation to Hallmark.

In the final version, Evans hears a sound emanating from his right. He reacts and looks in the direction of the sound, a dark and sinister-looking archway. He half draws his sword and says, "Who's there?" The camera swings slowly to Evans's right and then focuses in on the archway—a deep, spooky gray. There is movement, a huge shadowy figure moves forward and slowly comes into the dim light, pauses, steps forward—*it's Pat Weaver!* He smiles and says, "Hello, Mr. Hall, I'm Pat Weaver."

The effect was magical. Pat spoke with great charm and wit about "The Hall of Fame" concept. I presented the statistics and a merchandising program. We made the multimillion-dollar sale of a program that still survives.

There were other spectacular sales of Weaver ideas; one was called "Color Spread," an extension of the magazine concept. I sold the entire show to two sponsors, but my sales drive succeeded too well. When I brought in the orders, Pat looked at me sadly and said, "But Joe, that wasn't the idea of 'Color Spread.'" He didn't resist the new sponsors, but, within a season, I learned that Pat, once again, had been right in his concept. The idea was to have a one-hour color show with *nine* sponsors, so that the normal attrition per season would not wreck the commercial support. With nine different sponsors, ratings would not be so pivotal. To lose one or two of the nine would not be fatal, or even serious, since new sponsors would be gotten in time.

That concept worked for several years, and NBC was able to bring in sponsorship money in the millions despite some rating weaknesses. Those days with Pat Weaver were the happiest and most rewarding of my business life and incredibly instructive. I started at the lowest rung of management, at a salary of

$12,000 a year, and seven years later, because of the ability to analyze and persuade, I became president of the NBC Radio Network and executive vice president of NBC Television at an annual salary of $78,000 a year, plus bonuses.

A favorite persuader whom I have never met had the marvelous name Clarence Birdseye. There actually was one gentlemen responsible for the whole concept of frozen foods in the United States. Clarence Birdseye was that man. His life should be an inspiration to Billion Dollar Persuaders. He knew what was happening to America, saw the flight from the farms to major population centers, watched the development of refrigeration and the national transportation system: the railroads, the rapidly developing trucks, the improving roads. He had the capability of overview, and out of that capability emerged the concept of frozen foods.

Cyrus Curtis also knew what was happening in America. Railroads and network radio were making the United States a single community, though slowly. He believed that magazines would speed that process but by a vast educational process. He invested heavily in *The Saturday Evening Post* and spread its reach over the whole country, involving every community and almost every family through distribution by newsboys. He and his wife tested a page for women in *The Saturday Evening Post*, calling it "Woman's Journal." That became "Ladies' Journal" as it expanded. Eventually it became known as "The Ladies' Home Journal." It expanded, then outgrew *The Saturday Evening Post*, and became the famous, and astonishingly successful *Ladies' Home Journal*, which achieved a circulation of over seven million a month.

The late Norman Rockwell will rank forever with the greatest concept persuaders of all time. He answered my question about the genuine goodness he always portrayed in his illustrations (he refused to call himself a painter) with the explanation that when he left the protective environment of his own home and saw that the world had many evil, destructive and ugly aspects, he decided that he would ignore them and concentrate on the kindness, compassion, and humor of good, decent adults, the sheer beauty of the very young, and the character and tranquility of the old who have lived worthwhile lives.

His illustrations have been seen and enjoyed by more people than the works of all the great masters combined. Still, he was the target of criticism by those who said he was bland, socially unconscious, and used photographs in his work. He won my permanent affection and respect by saying, "My worst enemy is the world-shaking idea, stretching my neck like a swan and forgetting that I am a duck." That basic simplicity and self-mockery put Norman Rockwell above criticism, and he rolled along completing his beautiful illustrations of the good people and the less complicated aspects and traditional qualities of American life. He could, at the peak of his career, command large fees for his work. But for several decades he provided illustrations for the covers and stories in the official magazine of the Boy Scouts of America charging as little as $75 for an illustration.

He had a belief in human goodness and worth that became a mission-in-life. Norman Rockwell died at eighty-four, having won a kind of immortality rarely achieved. People will laugh and smile and cry and be warmed for centuries by the product of his heart, mind, and hands. Perhaps some young reader of this book, who has the budding ability to illustrate will be inspired to emulate Norman Rockwell. That would make all the effort put into this work a tribute to a very superior gentleman. Norman Rockwell wrote me a note in 1964 thanking me for saving the Curtis Publishing Company from bankruptcy and saving the jobs of ten thousand people who worked on the various magazines. He said he would like to do something for me. He asked, "Would you like me to paint your portrait?" I agreed, of course, and now consider my portrait by Norman Rockwell my proudest possession. It was the graciousness of the man, the kindness and compassion that now is immortalized in his thousands of paintings.

All the great concept persuaders have one quality in common: the capacity for overview. Some people have it instinctively, others acquire it. If you would aspire to high-level persuasion, you should regularly step back from the routine of your life. Mentally "go to the top of the mountain," and try to see the interrelationships of things and forces; it is in this frame of mind that you may see opportunities for persuasion for good causes that have been missed.

BDP Commandment 20 • **Recognize the difference between the *opportunity* to communicate and the *ability* to communicate.**

BDP Commandment 21 • **Recognize the difference between concept persuasion and product persuasion.**

BDP Commandment 22 • **Try to develop the capacity for overview, the knowledge and understanding of interrelationships.**

BDP Commandment 23 • **If you are unable to achieve the above, concentrate on product persuasion. (See Chapter Six.)**

✶✶✶

6

Product Persuasion

★★★★★★★★★★★★★★★★★★★★★★★★★★★★

During a business career spanning twenty-five years I tried to synthesize the science of marketing in a brief phrase or, by some miracle, one word. There have been as many descriptions of marketing as there have been describers, but I still failed to find the phrase or the word. However, once immersed in the research and writing of this book, I decided to make another attempt. The answer came after one of my daily meditation periods... and it was one word: *enhancement*.

Enhancement literally means "to raise to a higher degree, intensify, magnify." During the course of writing this book, as a challenge to myself, and a case history of persuasion, I am going to try to gain acceptance for this one-word description of marketing.

This chapter on product persuasion in contrast to concept persuasion will begin with a description of one of the most difficult product introductions and marketing drives in United States business history. It was the most expensive new product introduction up to that time, and it very nearly failed. That product was color television. The Billion Dollar Persuader, as in the case of radio and radio networking, was General David Sarnoff.

During his later years General David Sarnoff had little need of slow persuasion. He was one of the most powerful men in the United States, sitting atop the $4 billion Radio Corporation of America. He was powerful enough to place his son into the presidency of the corporation when he stepped back from its daily operation.

But it wasn't always thus. General Sarnoff needed all his powers of persuasion to hold the NBC Radio Network affiliates together while he blasted the news all over America that television was the wave of the future. The radio-only affiliates were understandably furious and some actually threatened to desert NBC. Sarnoff would not back down an inch in his honest appraisal of television, but he used his powers of persuasion to keep the affiliates in line. This was child's play compared to the problem General Sarnoff had in persuading his own organization—the distributors of the electronic world—and the American public that *color* television had arrived.

By way of comparison, imagine that any great leader preparing to persuade his stockholders, his own executives, and the public starts at ground zero. General Sarnoff started miles *below* ground zero because of a set of circumstances, some of which were the result of his success against his competitors, his frequent abrasiveness, and the "play it safe, play it small" natures of most of his executives. There were other circumstances over which he had little control. He couldn't control the other television set manufacturers to whom RCA wished desperately to sell color television tubes for their own, branded color television receivers. Sarnoff would have been delighted to see his competitors bringing out color television even without their buying RCA color tubes. He knew that RCA, dominating the black and white television receiver markets, would inevitably get its share of the color television receiver business as the market grew. But the market wouldn't grow at an acceptable rate if only RCA made color television sets.

The iron will of General Sarnoff was at the core of his billion dollar persuasion. A lesser man would have backed away from the monumental objections raised by almost everyone: the directors of RCA, the executives of NBC, the heads of all the major advertising agencies, and the major advertisers who knew the very small number of color television sets in the hands of the public. These advertisers knew that they would foot the bill for the development of color television in the early stages, though the public would ultimately get the bill in higher food and drug and other product costs. It wasn't always or even often a matter of gentle persuasion. The least of Sarnoff's concerns was the objections of the employees of RCA and NBC. A sure way to find oneself in the office of the hatchet man, arranging for severance pay, was to object to the development of color television.

A second major element of General Sarnoff's persuasion was the inimitable Sol Polk, the appliance retailer in the Midwest who, at times, sold about a quarter of all the major appliances sold in his area. He was a brilliant merchandiser, handling all lines of appliances, including television receivers. General Sarnoff used Sol Polk to break the united front against him. With great fanfare, it was announced that Sol Polk would mount a massive drive to sell RCA color television sets. A process started that gave momentum to the drive. Its second great push came from another brilliant Midwesterner, the president of the Admiral Company, Ross Siragusa. He, like General Sarnoff and Sol Polk, was a maverick. With inducements adequate to the task, Ross Siragusa agreed to enter the color television market, with a unit using RCA color tubes. Now, with two manufacturers and one massive retailer pushing color television, the atmosphere changed, though the dire financial picture darkened. It has been estimated that RCA spent $80 million to promote color television. I have always suspected that the true cost was twice or three times that, considering the time and energy that might have been employed elsewhere. Once again, the indomitability of General Sarnoff won over tremendous obstacles, the least of which was the unpredictability of the color sets themselves. Even in demonstrations attended by RCA engineers, the colors would bleed or go awry. The word-of-mouth condemnations of color television sets by irate owners was an incalculable negative that had to be overcome by a counterwave of favorable reports. The formula had to be just right. A good show in bad color would gain nothing. A bad show in beautiful color had no effect. What was needed, and finally came in the form of "Peter Pan," was a superb show in very good color. A few minutes' viewing of "Peter Pan," in glorious color overcame weeks and months of negativism.

Can you now imagine our world without color television? It might have been delayed for decades had it not been for that doughty Billion Dollar Persuader, General David Sarnoff.

The wildest possible contrast is the astounding story of Opium, which was launched in the United States as this chapter was in preparation. I suspect by the time this book reaches the bookstores, scarcely a man or woman alive will not have smelled Opium. On the off-chance that a reader or two might have been on a six-month nuclear submarine trip, Opium is a fragrance. It is the newest creation of Yves St. Laurent. The Paris correspondant of *Womens Wear Daily,* André Leon Talley, started his page-one, headline story on Opium with these words of Yves St. Laurent:

> I think the great success of Opium in Europe comes not only from the quality of the perfume but the scandalous mystery. It is mysterious. Men love to smell it on women. And there are some men who love to wear it. But the whole mystery comes from within my innermost thoughts, and my most personal expression I give to my work.

Womens Wear Daily gave the introduction of Opium nearly four full pages of its September 18, 1978 issue. The merchandising program for the introduction of Opium was unprecedented. One party alone, on a huge ship called the *Peking,* anchored in New York, cost about $250,000. The snob appeal was most artfully exploited by the listing, in a *WWD* editorial, of all the invited guests, with asterisks denoting the ready acceptees, who could be depended upon to appear at any party. This launching party was, of course, covered by the press, radio, and television, extending the editorial coverage of Opium across the entire United States.

This is what Pierre Berge, a key executive of the company, says about St. Laurent and Opium, with a straight face:

> Berge calls the Opium fragrance, "one of the most significant creative undertakings in the history of Yves St. Laurent." Noting he believes unequivocally in the unique creation of Opium, Berge added, "Anything Yves does is like a poet, an artist, a writer. When you see a dress of Yves', it goes beyond being a dress. So does Opium.
>
> "It expresses his inner thoughts. It is based on his entire philosophy, his sensibility toward life today, his romanticism."

And what does St. Laurent say about himself?

> There is no time for friends or my family. I love my family. I don't even have time to see my mother. Ten years ago, I had a huge open house for all my friends. Now, I think about them more often than seeing them. The last trip to New York, I hardly saw my friends who live there.
>
> Now is a bad moment to leave for New York. I lose so much essential time for fittings of the pret-a-porter.
>
> I hope to be able to see friends and enjoy New York on this trip. But it's always work. Now that I've reached maturity, at 42, in my work, it's the work that possesses me. And I am possessed by my work. This is at once sublime and awful.

Opium succeeded in Europe, it will undoubtedly succeed in the United States. Yves St. Laurent is truly a Billion Dollar Persuader. But isn't it sad?

There is an area in which concept persuasion and product persuasion meet. In other words, a man with a great concept applies it to already existing products and rides to glory. The best illustration I can think of to prove my point is London Fog.

Human beings have been wearing garments to protect them from the elements for thousands upon thousands of years. In modern times there have been hundreds of manufacturers producing raincoats and ponchos at prices ranging from a few dollars to several hundred, but there was no major worldwide brand of raincoat, and the business was divided among the many producers. Then a Billion Dollar Persuader came up with the idea of promoting selected raincoats under an evocative name. He selected the name London Fog because it had a built-in recognition factor with practically everyone in the Western world. Clever and professional advertising, merchandising and promotion exploded London Fog on the consciousness of the trade, and a sizable portion of the raincoats sold now bear the London Fog trademark: Big Ben. The concept was broadened to include other outergarments and London Fog is now considered one of the most successful promotions in history. And it is an American brand capitalizing on the London weather.

The field of toys and games has been peopled by some of the brightest and cleverest professionals in American business. Electronic toys and games will account for a large percentage of the total amount of toys sold in the United States. One Billion Dollar Persuader took an overview of the homes in the United States, and "seeing" the seventy million television sets already there, decided to capitalize on that household fixture by phasing in various electronic games that used the television receiver's power and screen. As this chapter is being written, in the fall of 1978, the toy and game industry is anticipating hundreds of millions in sales of television set-related games. Here again, it was the capacity for overview, the ability to interrelate existing products for a whole new source of commercial energy—and profit.

Product persuasion has become astonishingly more difficult in recent years because of the cost of new product introductions. A corporation like Bristol-Myers, producing drugs and cosmetics with a $3 billion-a-year volume now budgets at least $400,000 for the introduction of any new product during its test market phase. And that investment is made only to find out if they can then justify five, ten, or twenty million in a national commitment to the new product.

Most big corporations have a bureaucracy that makes it extremely difficult for a man with an idea to break through. One great corporate exception to this rule, for which I have enormous respect, tried to manage outside submissions by actually setting up a Department of Outside Submissions to which anyone approaching IBM would be referred. If the first contact was made by telephone, the very courteous manager of this department would explain the procedure, which first involved the signing of a statement that protected IBM from later lawsuits. Then a meeting would be arranged with the appropriate individuals at IBM who were in a position to accept and evaluate the idea. It sounded fine, but the procedure didn't work except in the protection of IBM. The top management became aware of the fact that almost no new ideas from outside were leading to new products or services. They decided to find out why, and a young marketing executive who had demonstrated quickness of mind and creative ability was assigned to the specific task of unblocking the channel of new ideas. There were several huge barriers to the success of this eager and talented young executive: there is what is known as the NIH Syndrome, NIH being an acronym for Not Invented Here; there is a reluctance among some middle management people to accept products and ideas from outside; and there is also the time lag between the acceptance of any product and its appearance on the market.

The history of the mood stone ring is a classic. It was initially successful, then, because several of the key people running the business organization were amateurs, all the momentum was lost, the competition flooded the market, and the market collapsed in less than nine months. The amateurs, including a certified public accountant and a charismatic "guru" type, learned too late the awful wisdom of the first commandment of the jewelry business: you may be first but you are never alone. This simply means that the nature of the jewelry business, the people in it, the concentration of manufacturing in Providence, Rhode Island, the interrelationship with the buyers in the major stores and chains, absolutely preclude the possibility of complete secrecy and exclusivity, even when patents are involved.

I was one of the founders of the Stress Transformation Center in which self-regulation training was taught to people suffering from stress-related ailments: migrane headaches, digestive problems, anxiety, excessive smoking and drinking, and weight problems. The mood stone ring was the development of a product for the public that resulted from the discovery that liquid crystal changed color with temperature changes in the body. It was as simple as that. We related that fact to the knowledge that people with cold hands were under stress. With self-regulation training these people could actually cause more blood flow to the hands, warming them. The mood stone ring reflected the increase in the hand temperature, with the stone turning from a cold black through various stages of dark brown, greenish blue, then purple. There was some tricky technology involved in the assembling of the rings themselves, although any good lab technician could examine the components and duplicate the technique. A West Coast inventor had some patents. The amateurs agreed to pay him a royalty for the exclusive use of the technique and innocently went ahead thinking they had some protection against competition. I recommended to management that they protect themselves in other ways, particularly by making alliances with the most notorious knock-off artists in the business, setting up controllable competition, and even taking a small percentage of the business done at lower prices by these "partners." The amateurs would have none of this.

The major commandments of this chapter relate to this last example discussed.

BDP Commandment 24 • **In certain businesses, like jewelry and fashions, remember, *you may be first but you are never alone.***

BDP Commandment 25 • **Patents and copyrights may be worthless in actuality; "knock-off artists" can set**

up a company, flood the market, and disappear by the time you can take legal steps.

BDP Commandment 26 • The best protection on a new product or new service is speed, momentum, and reasonable pricing.

BDP Commandment 27 • If competition is inevitable, set up your own competition by alliances with companies in the cheaper price ranges so that you discourage cut-rate competitors.

★★★

Whether it is concept persuasion or product persuasion, the moment of truth comes when the proposition is presented to the people who can make the decision. That is the subject of the next chapter.

7

Presentations
★★★★★★★★★★★★★★★★★★★★★★★★★★★★★★

Presentation Day is generally the culmination of a program of research, planning, contact, perhaps re-contact, and the limited victory of having the prospect agree to sit and listen to a specific or general presentation about the product or service. The *opportunity* to communicate has been achieved. From that point on the test is of the *ability* to communicate. They are different skills, The former is primarily administrative, demanding patience, but with ample room for creativity when the prospect is elusive. The latter is largely a creative process, which can, at times, make demands on administrative and mechanical skills.

There are countless ways of making presentations. In this area I am completely pragmatic; what works is good, what doesn't work is bad. Before going forward we assume that the preparation for the meeting has been adequate, that the audience—whether one person or many—can make the decision, and that there is no known bias against the product or service or individuals involved.

The following true story might amuse you. The late Fred

Horton, a senior marketing executive of NBC, boasted that there was "no buyer in America I can't get in to see." That two-decade record was threatened by an important executive who kept directing Horton to his subordinates. Stung by this "insult," Fred slipped by the receptionist, planted and lit a cherry bomb outside the reluctant executive's door, and stepped back. It exploded with an ear-splitting roar. The door flew open, the enraged executive stormed out, and then stared open-mouthed as Fred snapped, "There's nobody I can't get to see," and then stomped off.

I have to admit that I wouldn't want Fred Horton in a presentation meeting with *that* prospect!

One of my all-time favorite presentations, because it got the order for a $3 million annual investment in a television series, was made in a taxicab on the way from the United States Lines pier on the Hudson to the Waldorf-Astoria Hotel in midtown Manhattan. In the cab was Chief Wilson, the president of Alcoa, and Art Hall, the vice president in charge of advertising. He and Todd Hunt, the advertising manager, had patiently listened to my presentation as to why Alcoa should become a half sponsor of a one-hour dramatic show on NBC-TV. The amount of money was far more than anyone at Alcoa had ever contemplated, and no one executive—or even a combination—could make such a commitment. There wasn't much time, for Class A (7 to 10 P.M.) time periods were being gobbled up by the cigarette and drug manufacturers, and they were followed closely by the large food companies. The drug companies had a tremendous advantage because of the high-speed nature of that business and their absolute conviction that television was far and away the most effective way to sell headache remedies and laxatives. While the other industries were going about their usual slow pace, drug companies were grabbing up many of the best time periods. They wanted the top ratings and didn't much care about quality programming, as would Alcoa.

Art Hall had told me that Chief Wilson was on his way back to the United States by ocean liner. I suggested we meet him at the boat, having been told that hordes of executives, friends, and relatives were awaiting him at the Waldorf. Once he disappeared into that hotel he would be lost to me. With some misgivings, Art Hall agreed. We seized Chielf Wilson as he walked down the gangway and hustled him into a waiting cab. Art Hall introduced me, and explained the extraordinary circumstances of the television availability, and gave me the floor for the half-hour presentation of the values of the dramatic series, its rating forecast, and its merchandising power. Chief Wilson shook his head in amazement several times. When I mentioned the cost his initial amazement seemed minuscule compared to the comic double take he gave me and Art Hall. "Three million dollars! Take a lot of aluminum to get that back," he mused. Art Hall and I kept the pressure on this wonderful, old gentleman, and by the time we reached the Waldorf he said wonderingly, "Well, Arthur, this is a strange and unorthodox way to do business, but... go ahead." We shook hands on the $3 million deal.

Alcoa stayed with the sponsorship of "The Alcoa Theatre" for many years, ultimately spending at least $30 million in sponsorship and commercial expenditures. This success was the result of a combination of forces. I would literally go *anywhere* to make a sale. That gave me a tremendous advantage over my more sedentary competitors who wouldn't dream of deliberately booking a flight to a faraway city when it was learned that a good prospect was making the trip and could not be seen immediately any other way. I would and did, many times. Also Art Hall had learned that I would not embarrass him by making a foolish presentation to his boss. He also knew that I had a great deal of control over the promotion and merchandising arms of NBC. I would be able, he knew, to generate great support of Alcoa's advertising in merchandising. The story of this sale got around the inner circle and was partly reponsible for my reputation as a "tiger of a competitor."

Over the years I had exceptionally good results from luncheon presentations, particularly at the famed 21 Club on 52nd Street in New York. There was a good choice of rooms, starting with what was called Jack's Apartment. It was just that, a very tastefully decorated and furnished apartment in which drinks could be served, then lunch thereafter. There were other rooms for more formal or functional presentations. It would be no exaggeration for me to say that I persuaded hundreds of buyers to buy millions of dollars in products and services at the 21 Club. Most large cities have one or more restaurants that cater to businessmen and advertising men. But in smaller cities, very often the ideal place is a city club or a country club where business people gather for lunch.

One other club, The Pine Valley Golf Club in Clementon, New Jersey, shared my affections. This is the most beautiful, but most difficult golf course in America. It is a mecca for anyone who loves the game. I would take groups of up to sixteen golfers there for a long weekend, picking up the check for what was always a memorable experience. The food was simple but superb, the accommodations plain but comfortable. Business was never discussed during a weekend of golf, drinking, eating, and good fellowship, but hundreds of millions of dollars of television, radio, and print advertising flowed to my companies because of these weekends at Pine Valley.

Regarding technique and technology, I always involved myself in the early planning, I did not believe in being a judge, selecting what I considered the best of a group of alternatives. I felt I had an instinct for this area, and I wanted to be a leader, not just a judge. I sought ideas and suggestions but always asked a lot of questions about the audience, the personalities, the past history, and the competition we were likely to face.

The great advertising agency, BBD&O, pulled a switch on me after we had made a series of excellent presentations for their major radio advertisers. In order to educate their own people they asked NBC, CBS, ABC, and Mutual Broadcasting to make presentations on the same day. I thought long and hard about that, and won the day by getting Marlene Dietrich, Jack Benny, George Burns, and other talent on NBC Radio to come in live as a part of the NBC presentation. We wowed 'em!

What is a perfect presentation? One that achieves its objective, of course. That seems too simple, but during three decades in business I have witnessed far too many bad presentations resulting from preoccupation with technique and technology, rather than with content. One presenter became enamored of slide shows activated by voice cues. The speaker simply had to read the script. Key words in the script would trigger the projection's mechanism. The audience was much more interested in the gimmickry than in the content. Few remembered much about what was on the slides.

I suffered from an excess of zeal in one case and scared the hell out of an audience, the top management of NBC and almost a thousand NBC network affiliates. They had all read the trade press accounts of "Joe Culligan's Imagery Transfer Concept" and wished to know if there were applications to their local sales operations. I decided to make an imagery transfer demonstration the main general presentation. The presentation team was assembled and I gave out the assignments. I called for a dozen of the most dramatic sound effects, knowing that there were sound libraries both at NBC and elsewhere. Also, my sound engineers were the best in America. What they couldn't find, they would create. The presentation was given in the grand ballroom of the Waldorf-Astoria Hotel, late in the morning.

On the dais were Robert Sarnoff, Robert Kintner, and Harry Bannister of NBC, and members of the NBC Affiliates Committee. My introductory remarks were deliberately vague and scientific, and definitely puzzling to all but a few of the more sophisticated in the audience. Then, on cue, the lights went out, and for the next few minutes the room was filled with the most horrifying sounds of rape, murder, car and train crashes, explosions, collapses of buildings, racing fire engines, zooming aircraft, and unearthly electronic bubbles and squeaks. When the lights went up I realized that I had made a mistake. It was written in the white faces and startled eyes of my associates at the head table. I apparently had gotten used to the shocking sounds and had underestimated their effect. It took several minutes of soothing talk to get the audience back to normal. As the meeting ended, and the audience filed out, Harry Bannister said, "Jesus

Christ, Joe, why didn't you warn me?" and Bob Sarnoff asked "Joe, was it really necessary to turn the lights out?"

The closest we came to perfection at NBC-TV was with a children's show, "Ding Dong School." The incomparable Dr. Frances Horwich had developed a format that had instant success written all over it. Pat Weaver, despite his workload running the entire NBC operation, had time to consider children's programming. He opted for "Ding Dong School," which opened with Dr. Horwich ringing an old-fashioned, hand-held bell. She then talked to the assembled children, four years of age and up, like a gray-haired, portly, comforting, loving grandmother. The kids loved it. Their mothers loved it. It gave rise to the description of television as the "electronic baby-sitter." The kids would stay put in rapt attention for the duration of the program. We thought we had a sure winner, got our statistics together, then thought out what kind of general presentation we would have for a mass assault on the advertising agencies in all the major cities. The decision was made, as usual, by my choice of alternatives. This was a children's show, but the buyers were sophisticated, hard-nosed professional media buyers. The first presentation was at Young and Rubicam and was given by George Graham, one of the young men I had hired. He had with him just a large square box that he carried to the platform. As he started speaking, he lifted the outside container up and off, exposing an oversized children's building block on which was the letter "D." He took that off exposing the next block, which bore the letter "I," then the letters "N" and "G," and so on, simply placing the blocks in a row, which then spelled out DING DONG SCHOOL. The show's statistics and pertinent facts were on the other three sides of the cubes, which he exposed simply by turning the blocks to the audience. It was a most effective fifteen-minute presentation, topped off by George Graham's request for the order and the announcement that the blocks, with all the evidence of the value of "Ding Dong School," would be left for the media experts. We sold out the program, and it remained a great moneymaker for NBC in addition to gaining many kudos for the worthwhile nature of the show's content.

I put the idea away in my mental file and didn't use it again for about five years. I reused it in a totally different way during the first major meeting I was asked to run at McCann Erickson. The entire staff was brought into New York for a series of presentations. It was agency president Marion Harper's way of pulling the far-flung organization together. One of the first presentations, important in setting the tone of the meeting, was given by three brilliant creative men, all of whom were very, very bald. They sat on a raised platform facing the audience. I was the introducer and as I named each man, he lowered his chin, exposing the top of his bald head. The first bald head bore the word SELF. The audience chuckled. The second bald head bore the word DOUBT. The audience laughed. The third bald head said STINKS. The audience howled. Really great ideas never wear out, and adaptation can make presentations fresh and evergreen.

I was able to make one other contribution to that meeting. One of the most perplexing problems of our company was the failure to sell what we called the "two agency concept." McCann Erickson owned another advertising agency called McCann Marshalk. Nobody particularly liked the idea, and competition tried to use "lack of confidentiality" against us. I was the newest management arrival at McCann Erickson, and irreverent. I made the suggestion that since McCann Erickson owned an agency in London, called Pritchard Wood and Partners, that we talk only about "the *three* agency concept" on the grounds that as people heard about the three agency concept they would assume the two agency concept had succeeded. It worked.

For the starkest simplicity, however, I have to go back to my earliest days as a part-time, summer vacation canvasser for a company that made and marketed an insulating material called "bats." There was very severe competition in this field, most of it coming from a company that sprayed loose insulating fibers into the walls through a hose. (The theory was that the fibers would ultimately fill the space between the walls.) The salesman I was attached to was a jolly, comfortable gentleman in his mid-fifties, who was the star performer. I found out why in our first call together. I would start down one side of the street lined with houses, while he sat in his car reading the morning paper. I'd ring every bell, and when the housewife appeared, I'd give her a big smile and ask her if she read *Good Housekeeping Magazine*. If she said "yes," I would flip open the magazine to the full-page ad on our insulating product and ask her if she realized how much money she could save by improving the insulation in her walls and ceilings. If she hesitated a moment, I would say, "My manager is right down the street supervising an installation. Could I bring him to meet you, just for a minute, please?" About one in three would agree, so I would walk back to the car and get my "manager." In our first call together he used a hand prop, his own handkerchief, with dazzling effect. He simply took it out with a flourish, then folded it neatly in half, then in quarters, then in eighths, saying, "You see, Madame, our insulating material is exactly the same thickness throughout the entire square. The junk they blow into the walls falls by gravity, and sooner or later, it will all gather in the bottom of the walls. Ours always remains the same." It seemed to me that he sold every other prospect. That lesson in prop presentations was imbedded deeply, as was my first experience with "the averages" in selling, then later in marketing. On a block with sixty houses I would get one out of three to meet my "manager." He would sell one out of two. That would be ten sales per sixty homes. A sales manager could project that against the whole area, and judge potential and the number of salesmen necessary to cover the territory.

Hand props serve another vital function in meetings with new prospects who may be nervous or shy. They establish a focal point of mutual interest, getting the persuader and the prospect out of eye contact in the early stages of the meeting. If you are a salesman now, or a sales manager, take the time to think out whether you can introduce hand props into your sales equation.

Originality can often be a substitute for thousands of man-hours of research and tens of thousands of dollars in presentation costs. One of my favorite Billion Dollar Persuaders is Henry

Schachte, who had an illustrious career with Lever Brothers, the gigantic, worldwide producer of consumer products. After his retirement from Lever Brothers and the J. Walter Thompson advertising agency, he decided to start a golf club near his home in Connecticut. The fact that he had never done anything remotely like that bothered him not at all. His first move was an aerial survey in a small plane over the general area in which he hoped to develop his golf club. His practiced eye was attracted to a 200-acre tract with the required characteristics: hills, mounds, and sweeping meadows, properly angled for "dog legs," golfese for holes on which the second shots—and the third on par 5's would veer right or left for interest and variety. He ascertained its availability and price, got a gentleman's agreement, no-cost option, then selected the logical area for the clubhouse. Ideally, golf clubhouses should be on the ridge giving the most panoramic view of the whole course. He then selected the area for the eighteenth green, which should be seen from the terrace clubhouse. He brought in the local gardener, and had him mow the area of the green, leaving the unmowed portion as an outline for the green. He made a modest investment in a cup and a flagpole, with a fabric flag bearing the proud number 18.

The next step was the rental and erection of a gaily colored tent on the site of the clubhouse. He contacted his favorite professional golfer and gave him his instructions. The golf pro had a practice tee prepared near the tent, and directed the placement of markers at distances of 100, 150, 200, and 250 yards, on what was to be the first fairway.

Henry Schachte then directed the preparation of a simple presentation of the concept, details of membership, pricing, and applications for membership. He was ready for the persuasion phase. His "opening day" was carefully calculated to insure the best attendance of prospective members. The weather would be an important factor, both for esthetics and the very practical problem of parking, since all the prospects would drive their own cars. An area of easy access with excellent drainage was selected, mowed, and marked appropriately.

He secured lists of all the residents of the area within a twenty-minute drive of the site. Simple flyers were prepared and mailed or placed under the windshield wipers of the cars parked at the railroad station. Young boys were the willing deliverers. Scores of telephone calls were made to the most likely prospects, and Henry Schachte artfully secured news stories in the local newspapers. *He had spent less than $300 up to the opening day.* The land was later paid for out of first memberships and bank loans.

Fortune smiled on his enterprise; the weather on opening day was superb. The prospects flocked to the area, were directed smartly to the parking area, and arrived at the clubhouse tent smiling and very receptive to the presentation. Refreshments were served, then Henry Schachte opened the festivities, quickly introducing the pro, who gave a group golf lesson finishing with a marvelous demonstration. The written presentations were distributed, and a very low-pressure appeal was made for membership applications. Before the day ended dozens of applications were received, with checks covering the charter member membership fee.

During the next two weeks the word-of-mouth publicity spread over the area, more information was left in the cars parked at the stations, and the follow-up newspaper publicity, with pictures of the golf pro at the eighteenth green, worked its magic. By the end of the month, the membership rolls were filled, and the money was available for the design and building of the golf course. Within the second month the funds swelled sufficiently for the building of the clubhouse.

Originality had contributed mightily, but the magnificent result could not have been achieved without one other ingredient: the credibility of Henry Schachte.

A man in Utah, the late Joseph Valentine, accomplished an even greater feat of persuasion decades ago. He took a group of potential investors into the desert of Utah where there was absolutely nothing but sand and cactus and sagebrush. He gathered the group on a hill, pointed to a flat spot, and said, "I'm going to build the first independent oil refinery between

Pennsylvania and Los Angeles right here." His credentials from previous successes and his passionate authority convinced his prospects; the power of the idea was irresistible. He got the financial commitment from members of that group and, good as his word, did build the first independent refinery on that very spot. Tragically, after his death, a major oil company ruthlessly moved in on his widow and took the refinery away from the Valentine family.

In contrast was the most important presentation in the professional life of Thomas Murphy, the Prosecutor in the Alger Hiss Case. Americans have long had an addiction to courtroom dramas. It is understandable, particularly when life (or life imprisonment) and death are concerned.

Backed by admiration from his legal peers, Tom Murphy was credited with the major advantages of the prosecution over the defense in the notorious case of Alger Hiss. To this day, decades after his conviction, lawyers speak with reverence of the powers of persuasion which undermined the facade built by Hiss's defense council by the parade of character witnesses for the defendant. The horde was led by Dean Acheson, Secretary of State. Notable followed notable, stating that they had known and worked with Alger Hiss for years, even decades. Courtroom witnesses reported that they could feel the good will of the jury and the courtroom observers turn toward Alger Hiss as he sat, head bowed, accepting the praise and expressions of trust of men of impeccable reputation.

Prosecutor Murphy felt it too. He knew that the crisis had arrived. His problem was compounded by the poor appearance of Whittaker Chambers, the principal witness against Hiss. It is not known if he had planned his strategy in advance, or whether it evolved from his feeling of dismay and dread as with his character witnesses his opponent scored point after point. Now Prosecutor Murphy was going on trial before his peers, the press and the public. Could he rise to the challenge? He did. He became a "billion dollar persuader" by a brilliant strategy and highly effective delivery of his rebuttal after the parade of character witnesses for Alger Hiss.

He asked the jury to consider what would be happening if the defendant had been Judas Iscariot rather then Alger Hiss, during the investigations of the early Christians being led by Jesus Christ. He posed the question, "Who would have been the character witnesses of Judas Iscariot?" The other Apostles, of course, all telling the judges that they had known and worked with Judas for varying lengths of time, and certainly, wouldn't his principal character witness have been Jesus Christ, himself? His words fell like hammer blows on the jury and the observers. The mountain of sympathy for Alger Hiss melted away, while the physical evidence against him mounted. Alger Hiss was found guilty of perjury, imprisoned, and disbarred. The case has not been fully closed, and there are continuing attempts, one by the son of Mr. Hiss, to clear his name. The ultimate outcome of the case is anybody's guess, but Prosecutor Murphy that day and during the days thereafter, went down in legal history for his devastating rebuttal of the character witnesses of Alger Hiss.

Another extraordinary presentation was made in a courtroom by Harry H. Lipsig, known as the Kingpin of Negligence Lawyers. His client was Sara Allen, who was the plaintiff. The defendant, was Mae West. Sara Allen and Mae West had been good friends for many years. They even looked somewhat alike, when Sara Allen would make up and dress up a la Mae West. Sara Allen then decided to do a flattering impersonation of Mae West, and she did not object...until sometime later when Sara's act seemed to be too popular. Mae West decreed that Sara Allen cease and desist in the impersonation. Sara Allen sought legal advice, and selected Harry Lipsig to represent her in a suit against Mae West for a million dollars. Lipsig cross-examined Mae West and elicited from her her objections to the impersonation of Sara Allen. His summation became a classic, spread from one end of the country to the other.

> Can Sara's spinal undulations be subject to Mae West's regulations?
> For Mae now makes the claim of introducing sex to fame.
> Bumps and grinds and flirty songs all to antiquity belong
> And sex was known to Eve and Adam and hips before Mae West e'er had 'em.

In a much more serious vein, in negligence cases where his client was merely a passenger in a car and was injured, Harry Lipsig developed a technique which was surefire for his clients. He would simply put the driver of Car A on the stand to describe the accident. He would invariably blame the Driver of Car B. Lipsig would then put Car B's driver on the stand and he would or course, blame Driver A. It didn't matter much to Harry Lipsig which driver was guilty as long as the jury accepted either story, and gave his client a handsome award.

I had a delightful meeting with Harry Lipsig, in his office, which was beautifully decorated with pieces from various parts of the world, each with a charming story. But, when we started discussing negligence cases I could see why insurance companies feared this tiny, jaunty man. He had a missionary zeal about his clients, particularly when children had been injured.

In two other cases, in the Phillippines, Harry Lipsig gained judgements of a total of $625,000 for damages in two shark attacks on bathers. Plaintiff number one was the victim of the shark attack. There appeared to local attorneys to be no "cause of action." Harry Lipsig did his research and found that a swimmer had been attacked months before, and the hotel had not posted warnings. He also found that the hotel regularly threw garbage into the water near the beach. The case was settled out of court for $275,000 after Harry Lipsig's devastating presentation of his facts.

Another attack took place in the same area and this time the victim died. The widow's lawyers contacted Harry Lipsig. This case was settled for $350,000 for the victim's widow.

During his career, now spanning fifty years, Harry Lipsig has literally been a Billion Dollar Persuader, for some of his cases became the principal evidence for other lawyers in negligence cases in which jury verdicts and out-of-court settlements reached million dollar levels.

Demonstrations, either live or in television commercials, would seem to be the most effective way to sell products. Storyboards in magazines and newspaper advertisements follow closely in effectiveness. The basic reason is relatively simple.

Credibility is achieved by showing that the product does work and can do what is claimed for it. But some advertisers seek even more credibility by having well-known spokespersons putting their personal reputations on the line. The best of the spokeswomen was Betty Furness, who has demonstrated charm and intelligence and extraordinary staying power. Perhaps best known for her years with Westinghouse, she has become a consumer advocate, and a commentator on the NBC News staff.

Two magazines gave added credibility to their advertisers by awarding a guaranty seal to the products advertised in their pages: *Good Housekeeping* and *Parents' Magazine*. Year in and year out, *Good Housekeeping* carried more pages of advertising than any of its competitors. The *Good Housekeeping* Guaranty Seal contributed mightily to this fine record.

Long after achieving my billion dollars in persuasion of various kinds I concluded that there was still a deficiency in presentations. It is a distinct pleasure for me to now introduce to readers of this book my concept, "The New Communications Cycle." In its creation I have tried to practice what I preach in terms of 1) overview, 2) thorough research, 3) computer applications, 4) consideration of human dignity and human nature, 5) the uncertainty of human reactions, and 6) the importance of feedback.

New Communications Cycle [©]

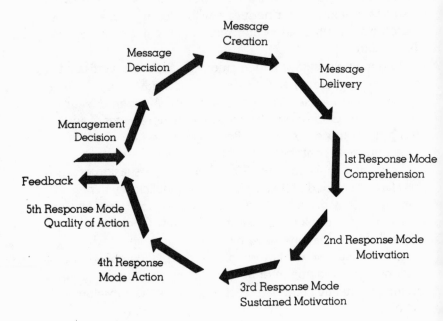

The New Communication Cycle starts with the decision of management to send a message to its organization or parts of its organization.

Once that decision is made the process starts. The message is created and the decision on just how the message will be presented is made. The range of choices is vast: print, motion pictures, animated films, recordings, slide shows, videotapes, skits, lectures, Q and A sessions, etc. The nature of the message, the nature and composition of the audience(s), time of day, day of week, even seasonal factors may be involved.

Then the message is delivered. In the past the management would then have to wait for weeks or months before knowing to what degree the message penetrated the audiences and caused the kind of action hoped for by the management when it made the original message decision. But the new system includes a patented computer-related method of mass response gathering and retrieval.

In the New Communication Cycle there are five response modes that will give management new, rapid feedback. Management can gain the assurance that the program has a chance to work because the message has 1) been comprehended by a large enough percentage of the employees, 2) the message has been motivational and has aroused interest and commitment, 3) the motivation is sustained among most employees, 4) the employees start taking the positive action, and 5) the quality of the action is of a sufficient level. The first advantage of the New Communication Cycle is the knowledge by the people who created and presented the message that their work will be evaluated very quickly by the response modes, and the quality of that work will improve. The next great benefit will be the option of the management to abort the program if the message is not comprehensible, motivational, and causitive of positive action at the required levels. The message can be rethought and redone immediately. If the program were evaluated in the old manner, whether success or failure, the time involved would be much greater.

If the program has been a success, and all five response

modes indicate that it is, then the feedback process continues. The successful program, in all its parts, goes into the memory bank of the management as a standard for future programs to be measured against in their conception and preparation.

It is my hope that the New Communication Cycle and accompanying Response Key system will be in use by one major corporation by publication date.

While this chapter was in final preparation I met a young persuader who opted for his own business rather than working for a large corporation. I found him very sympatico and alert to the many nuances of persuasion. Just as I had worked for a one-word description of the science of marketing, Ronald C. Tobias had labored mightily to visualize what he offered as a service to his clients and potential clients. The result of his efforts is shown here.

BDP Commandment 28 •	**In presentations the first three most important steps are research, research and research.**
BDP Commandment 29 •	**Seek the presentation that is most in harmony with the message, the audience and the physical setting. Do not let technique or technology overwhelm the message and facts.**
BDP Commandment 30 •	**Keep the formal articulation portion under thirty minutes if possible.**
BDP Commandment 31 •	**Do not overemphasize the obvious; accent the unique aspects, if any.**
BDP Commandment 32 •	**Ask for the order at the close of the presentation.**

BDP Commandment 33 • Leave behind a written and/or illustrated summary of your presentation.

BDP Commandment 34 • See if the New Communication Cycle© can be adapted to your presentation needs.

★★★

The Marke

How to fit the pieces together?

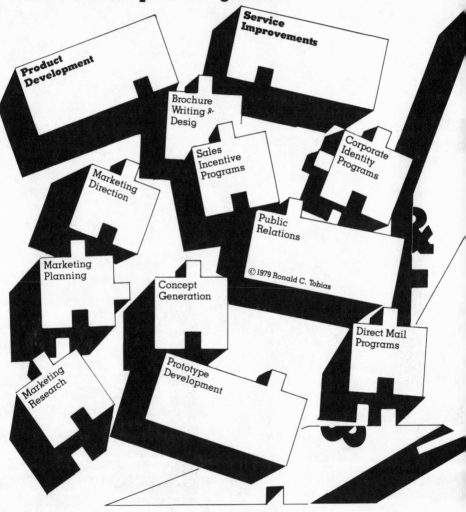

Service Improvements

Product Development

Brochure Writing & Desig

Sales Incentive Programs

Corporate Identity Programs

Marketing Direction

Public Relations

© 1979 Ronald C. Tobias

Marketing Planning

Concept Generation

Direct Mail Programs

Marketing Research

Prototype Development

ing Puzzle

**Marketing Mechanics'
Unified one-stop solution.**

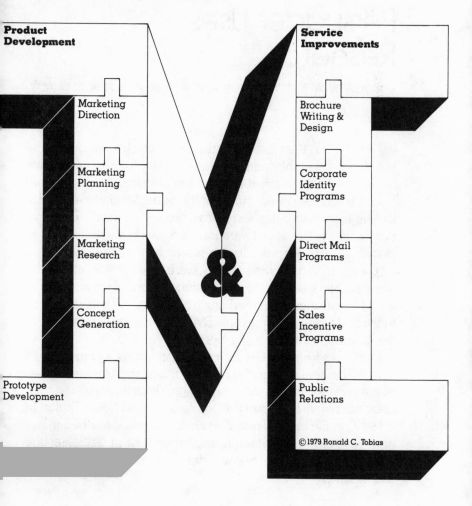

Product Development
- Marketing Direction
- Marketing Planning
- Marketing Research
- Concept Generation
- Prototype Development

Service Improvements
- Brochure Writing & Design
- Corporate Identity Programs
- Direct Mail Programs
- Sales Incentive Programs
- Public Relations

© 1979 Ronald C. Tobias

8

How the Billion Dollar Persuader Uses Research

★★★★★★★★★★★★★★★★★★★★★★★★★★★

At an award ceremony at which I was one of the recipients, I was introduced by a very dear friend, many years my senior, who shocked me and the audience by saying that "Joe Culligan is a fraud. He is *not* the best salesman in America. But he is probably the best *researcher* in America." This gentleman knew my secret weapon as a marketing executive in pursuit of a major sale. It was research of such volume and efficiency that my presentations were often irresistible to the prospect because of the overwhelming nature of my knowledge about his business. I learned much about research from various individuals, one of whom was Dr. Frank Stanton, president of the Columbia Broadcasting System.

During its formative years, broadcasting was a young man's game. The demands on the nerves, brains, muscles, and digestive system were such that only tough, disciplined, young men could survive the rigors of the business. Robert Lewis Taylor, in a 1947 profile in *The New Yorker,* accurately described thirty-nine-year-old Frank Stanton, then president of CBS, as "the boy wonder in a field of boy wonders." His principal initial talent was research

Frank Stanton was born in Muskegon, Michigan, in March 1908. He had a great innate interest in mechanical devices, but he had a creative side as well, getting involved early in photography, newspapers, printing, and poster art. He had an opportunity to exercise these talents in a department store job in Dayton, Ohio, which he had to take to earn spending and dating money. He became a gadfly, buzzing about, getting into everything, and getting more responsibility as his talents were recognized.

Stanton entered Ohio Wesleyan, a Methodist university several hours' driving time from Dayton; he studied business administration, then switched to medicine, and finally settled on psychology. And psychology led Stanton to a consuming interest in behavior, and that meant research. He may have been among the first researchers to start discounting verbal research data, that is, the data gained in face-to-face or telephone interviews.

This conclusion may have stemmed from the discovery, made very early in the study of psychology, that human beings often can't, won't, or don't admit their true feelings about many subjects. It was also known that introverted people avoid interviews when possible and, when trapped into one, seek to terminate the agony as expeditiously as possible. These findings indicated that there were serious flaws in the results obtained from canvassing and direct interviews.

Take, for example, Oak Street in a town in Westchester. The houses are nicely spaced, each owner having good visibility of the nearby homes. Our researcher, working on a magazine advertisement penetration study, drives up, parks his car, and heads for the first house. The woman either accepts or rejects the invitation to have the stranger "ask a few questions about magazine advertising."

Most people are courteous and cooperative in general, so it is reasonable to assume that those who say "no" are shy, introverted women. Therefore, Conclusion No. 1 is that most of the interviewees reached in this manner are extroverted. Consequently, the "facts" gathered by the researchers, even assuming that the respondents tell the whole truth, represents data not of a sample of all housewives, but a sample of *extroverted* housewives. Stanton, as a psychologist, would know that an extrovert would probably have a different life style than an introvert. It could follow that advertising appeals would not have the same effect on an introvert as they would on an extrovert.

Then there is the "fatigue factor," not recognized until years after the acceptance of "reader research." Consider the woman, extrovert to be sure, who agreed to an interview to discuss the effectiveness of magazine advertisements in *Good Housekeeping* (300 pages thick) and *Ladies' Home Journal* (175 pages). The woman is cooperative, even though she is busy, and she dutifully answers the questions. "Did you see this ad?" If "yes," the ad is "noted"; the second question leads to a "seen associated" vote; the third, records the "read most" vote. The respondent, now getting bored, learns quickly that if she says "no" to the first question, the interviewer turns to the next page. If she says "yes," she get two more questions. If she really wants to terminate the interview without being rude, she says "no" to each question and gets through each one in one-third the time. Some proof of this was accomplished by *Good Housekeeping*, which resented its lower ratings compared to the *Journal*. The fatigue factor was dimly perceived by someone and it was believed that this was hurting the thick *Good Housekeeping* far more than the less ad-populated *Journal*. A clever method was devised to prove that the fatigue factor was affecting the results.

In the first test, instead of using a regular issue of *Good Housekeeping*, special issues were "thinned down" to the same size as the competitive magazines. The *Good Housekeeping* scores increased—or so the researcher said.

A second method was used to approach the problem a different way and also to solve a problem created by advertisers. Advertisers demanded "front-of-the-book" positions because the readership studies indicated that ads placed there, rather than in the middle of the back, had greater visibility. The clever devils at *Good Housekeeping* had the researcher start his questions from the back cover toward the front instead of the usual method of front cover toward the back. Eureka! Again success—the scores on the ads in the back increased, again proving the fatigue factor.

Dr. Frank Stanton understood very early that the researcher knows more and knows it earlier than anyone else in his world. With such knowledge, he can have a huge advantage if he has amibitions beyond his field or department. Exclusive knowledge, of course, would be devastating, but there rarely is such a freak, since all modern organizations maintain extensive research activities.

Frank Stanton, a junior in college, was one in a million, for he designed, built, installed, and maintained a nonverbal research tool and had its exclusive use for his own purposes long enough to make his first breakthrough into broadcasting (then only radio) in 1931.

Stanton discarded the verbal research techniques and created the first nonverbal, mechanical device to automatically record the listening activities of the home radio user. It was accomplished by the installation, inside the radio set, of a simple device with a motor, moving tape, and timer. The on/off switch activated the timer and tape, and the dial selector "told" the tape what station was being listened to and for how long. This was, three years later, to be his "gimmick," his key to the Columbia Broadcasting System. This was probably the most important lesson in his young life: to know something valuable first and use it for leverage. Part of the business life style of Frank Stanton was his action cry, "Let's find out."

Ratings after-the-fact were, of course, important. But Dr. Frank Stanton envisioned something far more dynamic and useful: a method of determining in advance how a radio and television program was likely to perform after it did get on the air. Under his direction CBS developed a "program analyzer" that now seems simple and logical, but was very advanced for its time. Groups of people were invited into screening rooms at CBS and shown vignettes of programs and various actors and actresses. They had a simple set of buttons to press that indicated their favorable, unfavorable, or neutral reactions to what

they were viewing. By consolidating these votes, the CBS programming executives could literally try out situations, dialogue,
and actors and actresses in this living laboratory setting. Better
programs reached the CBS audience, and there were less fail-
ures. It didn't always work; some competitor going purely on
instinct would come up with a winner, but the record of CBS's
rise to Number One was heady evidence that Dr. Frank Stanton
was right.

I learned about research as a weapon of persuasion very early
in my business career. I gained attention of top management in
my first postwar job at *Good Housekeeping* by researching
aspects of this publication outside the areas of circulation and
readership. I found that *Good Housekeeping* had an identification with millions of women through its *Good Housekeeping*
Guaranty Seal. Millions of *Good Housekeeping* cookbooks had
been sold and were in daily use in a significant portion of
American kitchens. There were millions of merchandising signs
in retail stores all over the country stating "As Advertised in
Good Housekeeping." *Good Housekeeping* editorials were
quoted in women's pages of countless newspapers all over the
United States. Gathering all these statistics I created what I
called "the *Good Housekeeping* area of influence," using a
technique that was visually stunning. The presentation started
with just the cover of *Good Housekeeping Magazine* tastefully
displayed. Little did the unsuspecting audience know that by the
use of panels hidden behind the cover I was able to bring
exhibits out on the left, right, top, and bottom, in an ever
increasing display. By the time I was finished, the three million
circulation of *Good Housekeeping* had been supplemented by
the millions of "extensions" of *Good Housekeeping,* making
the total area of influence look enormous. This was important
because *Good Housekeeping* had the smallest basic circulation
in its field.

In every management role I was fortunate enough to fill I used
research to the ultimate. The one organization in which I
found it the most difficult to make a contribution was the
McCann Erickson agency, which was the "milk cow" for the

burgeoning Interpublic, Inc. It was the commitment of Mr. Marion Harper to make Interpublic the world's first worldwide communications complex performing services to the super corporations of the world in advertising, public relations, merchandising, sales promotion, sales training, recruitment, television and radio programming, trade, government, and consumer relations. The research people at Interpublic were so outstanding that I found it almost impossible to come up with anything not already thought of and done, or suggested and rejected. But I persisted. "Share of market" research was very big at that time, and there were good and improving services on which advertising agencies and their clients could depend for accurate information on "how am I doing" in the retail stores vis-à-vis competition. I knew it was good, but I sensed that it was not going far enough. So, I thought out what I described as "Share of Mind vs. Share of Market Research." The rationale was simple. The public bought products for a number of reasons, some having little to do with product satisfaction. Convenience, availability, price, color, packaging, positioning on shelves, etc., all contributed. My question addressed itself to the question, "What does the consumer *really* think of your product?" It seemed plain to me that if the consumer gave a product a high rating on Share of Mind, the only reason he or she would buy the lesser-rating competitors product was retail availability or a lower price.

Conversely, if the consumer had a low opinion of the product, but still was buying it, it wouldn't be long before he or she would switch to a product that had a better Share of Mind rating. Share of Mind vs. Share of Market Research became a very useful weapon for Interpublic's clients and also a very sharp advantage in the constant new business activities.

There is a negative side to the whole area of research in the United States, The list below is a summary of developments of the last decade.

1. Good research has become very expensive. Bad research is the most expensive of all.

2. The number of people who do their work well has steadily diminished. There are individuals in the research field who are not dependable or honest.

3. It is still possible to get *initial* opinions from consumers; but second and third responses have been difficult to impossible to assume. So the "tracking" of progress, which is so important to a keen management, is becoming more difficult and expensive.

4. Ultimately, the research data is only as good as the evaluation and interpretation of it. That is another capability that has deteriorated generally.

5. Research has become a multitude of specializations with the attendant confusions. The entry of computerization into research has led to an excess of systems thinking by technicians. (Frustrations with his computer research led a friend of mine, president of an oil company, to snarl, "All I want to know is what time it is, and you insist on telling me how the watch works.")

Like it or not, computers are and will henceforth be an essential part of the life of the Billion Dollar Persuader. Computers were first sponsored in industry by financial people and scientists, who saw how computers could liberate them from the drudgery of calculations in one fraction of the time needed by teams of individuals using conventional calculators.

Be warned about letting yourself be trapped into process orientation by computer technicians. Look at computers this way. You can walk into your garage, get behind the wheel of a thirty-thousand-dollar Mercedes, start it and drive a thousand miles without understanding a damn thing about what's under the hood. If you develop mechanical trouble, you take the car to a "process-oriented" service station. The same can be true about computers. You, as a Billion Dollar Persuader, can use a computer system by knowing just a small percentage of the facts about these wonderful machines. Don't call in your specialists and ask them to give you a system. You decide what end results you want for your decision-making process, and tell them to come back with the answers *you* want, not what their system wants to give you.

The New Communications Cycle© should be highly interrelated to computer technique and technology for mass responses. For example, a corporation like Monsanto Chemical has about eighty thousand employees. It is not inconceivable that the management may wish to create and deliver a message to all eighty thousand employees and measure the levels of comprehension, motivation, sustained motivation, action and quality of action by using the Response Modes© that are the unique advantage of the concept. By computer, the responses can be gotten on data cards that can be processed very rapidly. In addition, by designing a program properly, the changing attitudes of employees can be "tracked" as subsequent responses come in for evaluation.

While this book is in preparation I am launching a new research service with a friend who took early retirement from IBM. The thrust of our new concept is a vast improvement in the commercial television rating services, which, in my opinion, have been woefully inaccurate in qualitative audience measurements. This decade-long and continuing inadequacy has inevitably led to the pandering of commercial television to the lowest common denominator of public tastes.

The odds are against anyone confronting a bureaucracy, even a Billion Dollar Persuader can't win 'em all. I was amazed at the negative reaction of the professional researchers at two of the three commercial networks. They did not seem to want any changes in the television rating services. After probing deeply, and encouraging argument and debate I found that there seemed to be a conspiracy of silence about sampling methods. In every discussion the old cliché about the blood sample giving all the evidence needed about the condition of the whole body was offered as justification for the present sampling methods. At the critical point in one meeting I simply asked, "Will a blood sample tell you the condition of the patient's teeth?" There was an embarrassed silence.

I decided to do something about the conspiracy of silence among professional researchers. I went first to Dr. Frank Stanton, the patron saint of all television researchers. I told him of the resistance I had met and the wall I encountered when I raised questions about the sampling techniques. He admitted in his typical penetrating way, that current sampling methods would not lead to qualitative measurements.

That was my whole premise, so I took the next step. I dropped a small bomb in the leading advertising industry magazine, *ANNY*. The story read:

CITIZENS RESPONSE: REFINING TV RESEARCH

Matthew J. (Joe) Culligan, who is known to many in the trade as a professional president (he was president of such firms as Curtis Publishing Co., the NBC Radio Network, Mutual Broadcasting Co., and Teletape), has turned his creative eye on a different field: research. Along with his partner, Ed Corwin, an early IBM marketing retiree, he has formed a company called Citizen's Response which is aiming to refine existing research methodologies, in particular, the TV research field.

"People complain all the time about the need to improve the quality of TV programming," Culligan said. Now with the new system Citizen's Response is devising, he said, "these people will be able to do something about it." He hopes to interest the networks in the system.

Our society's more highly educated people, Culligan maintains, do not generally become involved as subjects in TV research, primarily because of their dislike for "keeping diaries or electronic devices in their closets," as other existing research methods require. As a result, TV programming has been, by and large, dictated by the people who do take part in research studies; people whose programming tastes, do not, presumably, coincide with the more highly educated and "form the most exclusive club in the world (to) improve the quality of TV programming."

Citizen's Response, which has already conducted research for politicians, TV shows, and the Department of Housing & Urban

Development in the state of Washington, is now turning its antennae to TV research. "We want to supplement existing TV research, replace some of them with the net effect of making (all methodologies) better," Culligan said. The electronic research system utilizes what he calls the Response Key, a moneysaving device in the form of a patented template which stores information on a card instead of in the computer. The set-up is designed to elicit second, third, and fourth responses to questions as an aid to tracking public opinion.

The reaction was not long in coming. "Culligan is ripping up the peapatch again," was one unamused reaction from an old adversary. That I was, and I determined to continue my assult on the bastion of the professional "inner circle" research directors of the commercial television networks. I had done my best to gain their cooperation and been rebuffed. It was the kind of situation that had me sniffing, like the old fire horse, for trouble. Perhaps I will some day be able to report on some success in breaking the stranglehold of the present television rating services and end the conspiracy of silence about sampling methods.

BDP Commandment 34 • **Sales can be predetermined by the volume and quality of research achieved.**

BDP Commandment 35 • **If there is existing research which favors your competition, test it vigorously for its validity.**

BDP Commandment 36 • **Do not trust verbal research; some people cannot or will not tell the truth.**

BDP Commandment 37 • **Explore nonverbal research techniques.**

BDP Commandment 38 • **Good research is expensive; no research can be more expensive; bad research can be the most expensive of all.**

BDP Commandment 39 • Computers and programs for information gathering, storage, and retrieval are absolutely fundamental to the Billion Dollar Persuader.

BDP Commandment 40 • Resolve and train yourself to be result oriented, not process oriented, in dealing with computers.

★★★

9

Follow-Up, Getting the Order, Avoiding Overkill

★★★★★★★★★★★★★★★★★★★★★★★★★★★

In order to get from the magazine business to television I was advised to break into the commercial motion picture business, make the necessary contacts, then haunt the offices of the marketing directors of the three networks. I thanked the good Lord regularly that I had the move to television as my ultimate goal. The commercial motion picture business, at that time, was a dreadful morass. There was wheeling and dealing, direct and indirect payola, nepotism, price cutting and plain dishonesty. I was determined to play it straight, believing that ultimately the good guys would win out. I went to work as the Eastern Division Vice President of John Sutherland Productions.

I set about my task of getting motion picture assignments with vigor and my usual enthusiasm, using some marketing techniques not normally employed in this business. I created many opportunities to communicate by setting up screenings of our work, either entire films or what we called our "demonstration reel," excerpts of our best work.

Time after time we lost out to competitors, some of whom not at all at our level of writing and production. Gradually I got the message. Almost every company in the field in New York was operating below the table. Girls and drugs were sometimes used as inducements to buyers. I redoubled my efforts to get into television, and fortunately was hired by NBC-TV before too much damage was done to my ego. I tell this tale to warn young people to avoid businesses that are not entirely legitimate. There the Billion Dollar Persuader can literally do everything right, and still not get the amount of business he deserves.

Assuming therefore, that the business is legitimate, we come to the critical area after the opportunity to communicate and the ability to communicate have been successfully negotiated. The presentation(s) have been made, and the most difficult stage for the persuader has arrived. There is the immediate decision about follow-up. Should it be done with printed material handed out after the presentation? That is generally a very good idea if the presentation is done in the client's facilities. One of the most effective follow-ups in my experience was when the presentation was made at the 21 Club in New York. The group assembled for drinks and lunch, all neatly accomplished by 1:15. The presentation was made after the main course, before the dessert and coffee. It was deliberately crafted for a maximum of twenty minutes, with ten minutes for questions, if any. During the lunch twenty messengers picked up presentation kits at NBC and rushed throughout New York City delivering them directly to the desks of the ladies and gentlemen who were at the luncheon. We got an excellent reaction to that, and did it several more times, quitting when the law of diminishing returns set in with imitators.

However, a near disaster made every one very cautious about the delivery of gimmicks to clients and prospects. A hillbilly show on NBC daytime TV was promoted with the delivery of bottles of apple cider to advertising agency executives. The problem was, the fermentation had not been complete. Cider bottles exploded in desks, coat closets, and file cabinets until emergency squads got the bottles back. NBC paid a healthy cleaning bill for this idea!

It is difficult to think of a case in which some written or visual follow-up can be safely ignored. If competition is severe, the reinforcement of the message given in the presentation is doubly important, particularly if the competitive presentation follows yours. *Last* impressions are vitally important. This is important enough for follow-up to be a matter of policy.

Asking for the order should also be a matter of policy for a sales and marketing organization. There are unusually good ways of encouraging buyers to make commitments. I had the pleasure of introducing the Charter Client Plan to the broadcasting business. To develop a sense of urgency about "The Tonight Show" with Steve Allen, I designed this plan that promised very special advantages to advertisers who would sign contracts before a certain cut-off date. For making an early commitment the client got such benefits as rate protection, a special free merchandising package, preferred position for commercials and other extras. The "Tonight Show" Charter Client Plan worked too well, leading me to the conviction that the advertising rates were too low. We sold the show out immediately, and irritated some good potential customers who simply could not be accommodated.

Increases in the prices of goods and services are also an excellent method of stimulating prospects to make commitments early. Price protection for a set period of time can be promoted as the very best good business reason for signing contracts before deadline dates. (Rate protection was an important feature of the Client Protection Plan.)

Over the decades the best "follow-uppers" and "closers" have been insurance salesmen. The very good ones have a missionary zeal about them, having convinced themselves that the entire transaction of selling you insurance is a service for the good of humanity. They have the advantage of pushing prospects pretty hard on behalf of widows and orphans: *your* widow and *your* orphaned children.

Bluntly, overkill is not knowing when to shut up. There is a point at which aggressiveness is counterproductive. This is a matter of individual judgment, but there are some tricks of the trade that can be helpful, and here's one. The persuader can go as far in follow-up and asking for the order as he dares. He backs away for a few days, then invites the prospect for lunch or dinner; or golf or tennis if appropriate. The invitation can be social, but the odds are that the possible client will try to have some kind of an answer for the host at a pleasant lunch; he may well give an answer without being asked.

It is generally true in life that no one will put a higher value on an individual than he puts on himself. This is very true in business. The total image you project in personal grooming, dress, speech and gestures and professionalism will have a great deal to do with the reception you get from secretaries, receptionists, assistants, and decision-making prospects. If you project a sense of dignity and propriety you will generally get a reaction in the same mode. I tried and generally succeeded in projecting an image of success and expectation of affirmative responses to my presentations. I rarely encountered rudeness or lack of consideration, but when I did, I never responded in kind. During one presentation one of the people in the audience started whispering to a colleague on his right. The third time he did it I stopped, smiled at him, and did not continue until he had stopped whispering. He repeated the act, I stopped again, and smiled at him. But his associates became irritated and after a few dirty looks he stopped his distracting actions. You should resolve to look, think, act, and speak in a manner that demands respect.

BDP Commandment 41 • **Stay out of or get out of unethical or cutthroat businesses.**

BDP Commandment 42 • **Gimmicks can be a two-edged sword. Be prudent.**

BDP Commandment 43 • **Develop inducements to speed up commitments, such as Charter Client Plans, price increases, rate or cost protection.**

BDP Commandment 44 • **Dress, speak and act in a manner that commands respect.**

10

Public Speaking

★★★★★★★★★★★★★★★★★★★★★★★★★★

During my years as a "professional president," as I have been jokingly called, I accepted many invitations to speak at colleges and universities. Officially, I said it was because I enjoyed being with young people. Enjoying the golf courses nearby would have been a more accurate description, but there was another reason for acceptance. I enjoy being before groups, assured of their attention and admiration if my speeches were good enough. In one case, at the University of Florida, my first speech was good enough to get me a second invitation. Then I received a third and a fourth. When the call came about coming back for yet another appearance, I had an unusual attack of modesty and said something about "wearing out my welcome." Ten days later a large tube arrived from Jacksonville, Florida. In it was a long, continuous, round robin letter urging me to come back, signed by over a hundred students of the Communications School. I decided to give this audience more than just a speech. Without telling anyone other than my host, who was head of the Communications School, I arranged for a worldwide closed circuit broadcast—*live*—from London, Paris,

Tokyo, and Bonn. On cue I called in the very well known NBC foreign correspondants in those cities and engaged them in a brief chat, then asked them to give a summary of what was going on politically and in the entertainment world. The presentation was an absolute smash.

Portions of their reports to the Jacksonville audience were taped and used by NBC in the regular news shows, so the expense was minimal. I asked that there be no publicity about this presentation, so I was able to use it several other times with equally good effect.

It was particularly effective in Toronto when I was asked to be the principal speaker at the conference of newsmen of the North American broadcasting industry. This was always a testing audience, being a combination of writers, editors, and on-the-air reporters and commentators. Getting off to a good start was particularly important, so I asked my good friend Chet Huntley for a story having to do with the newspaper business. He gave me this beauty:

> The late, great newspaper publisher, Joseph Pulitzer, had a routine which was religiously followed by his editors. After the initial screening and interviews, all aspiring applicants for jobs in editorial at the *St. Louis Post Dispatch* were referred to this awe-inspiring gentleman. He would always puckishly end his interviews with women applicants with this admonition. "Remember, my dear, truth to a newspaper is like (pause for effect) virtue to a lady".
>
> One of the recipients of this caution replied, "That may be true, Mr. Pulitzer, but a newspaper can always print a retraction."

This particular story had everything for that audience. The name and reputation of Joseph Pulitzer and the *St. Louis Post-Dispatch,* a bit of double entendre.

Almost as successful was this story for the faculty of a major college. Here again, this was not the easiest group to capture. It went:

> A student at Oxford was crossing the campus when he saw his favorite professor busily engaged in pumping air into one of the tires of his bicycle. As he got closer he saw that the savant was pumping the air into the front tire, which was quite sound. The rear tire was the flat one. When the student pointed this out, the professor said, with mild astonishment, "Oh, I say, don't they *communicate?*"

Not exactly my idea of a belly laugh, but right for that particular audience. And that is the key. My most recent success was during a speech before an audience of scientists in various branches of genetics, psychology, and psychiatry. I advised the group that I was going to tell them the story of the Amorous Italian.

> A group of anthropologists discovered and captured the first white, hairless orangutan in the jungles of Borneo. They return to England, filled with awe and wonder. These emotions wear off in six months and one of the British scientists thinks the unthinkable and timorously suggests that they try to mate the orangutan with a human being, forever solving the mystery of the missing link. They decide to go forward, very mindful of the complex political and moral questions involved in this experiment in human engineering. They decide to run some discreet advertisements in male, macho publications, in each case using the enticing headline: $10,000.
>
> They receive several hundred inquiries, which are carefully screened for the half-dozen most likely prospects. The six are further screened in personal interviews and three are decided upon as the final candidates from which the one perfect man will be selected. The committee finally does select one man to whom the committee writes outlining what they expect of the participant. They then ask for a list of his conditions. His letter, apparently written with counsel, sets out the following conditions for his assent:
>
> 1. There be no publicity.
> 2. My wife must never know.
> 3. There will be no kissing on the lips.
> 4. Any offspring will be raised as Catholics.

5. I must have thirty days to raise the $10,000.

Getting off to a good start with any audience is such an obvious advantage that I need not linger on the point, other than to confirm that first impressions are very important. Last impressions are also very important, but one I created at a huge meeting in the grand ballroom of a major New York hotel was slightly embarrassing. I had acted the MC for three days, getting performers on and off the stage with great precision. At the end of the final meeting, after introducing the man making the closing remarks, I missed a step and fell off the stage. The speaker quipped, "That Culligan, he'll do anything to attract attention!"

In one speech I faced a particularly knotty problem because of the combination of creative and artistic types plus financial and administrative types in the large audience before which I appeared as the banquet speaker. There was much I could have said, personally, but at the time I was the chairman of the board of a very large company, though I also had excellent credentials in the creative and artistic areas. However, that reputation had receded as the promotions to higher levels of management came my way. I reasoned that a bias to business would be assumed by the artistic and creative people, regardless of any attempts to appear to be a fair arbiter.

The speech was made at the time "Hazel" was a very successful television series. The character, Hazel, was the creation of Ted Key who supplied episodes for television while also doing his cartoons for *The Saturday Evening Post*. I decided to make him my advocate, telling him of my personal dilemma. I asked him for a brief opinion on the relationship of creative people and those in financial-administrative roles in business life. I quoted his memo verbatim, and I reproduce it here not only as an example of a way to work around a difficult audience, but also because it is sensible. Whether the persuader is in the creative, administrative, engineering, or financial realms of business, there is much to think about in the following couple of hundred words.

To: Joe Culligan
From: Ted Key

Some Thoughts on the Relationship
Between Creative People and the Financial World

Perhaps I'm wrong, but it seems to me that the gulf between creative people and the financial world is really one of semantics. If artist would only call themselves VISUAL ENGINEERS, and the financiers, ECONOMIC SCULPTORS, our problems might be solved. But the picture's a bit cloudy. Mention artist to many and they see an unreliable clod of neuroses growing a beard. Let the artist hear the word finance and what springs to mind? Moneybags and fat cigars. A few words, images, and meanings have to be changed.

As a matter of fact, creative people and financial people are really much alike. All the successful creative people I've known have been purposeful, resourceful, farsighted, industrious, talented and imaginative. All the successful financial people I've known have been purposeful, resourceful, farsighted, industrious, talented, and imaginative. They do different things differently, yet in the same way.

And both seem to know that self-interest is best served when it contributes to the self-interest of others.

That's been my experience, anyway. All my life, the harder I've worked for others, and they for me, the richer we both became. Richer in the best sense of the term, for ourselves and for the community.

I created "Hazel" and *The Saturday Evening Post* has published it for over twenty-one years. The Curtis Publishing Company has spent a great deal of money on the cartoon's exposure. And I've invested years of my talent and time. We share the rewards as equal partners, from the "Hazel" show and many other "Hazel" activities. Without each other, there would be NO rewards. Curtis believes in its creative people and puts its money where its mouth is. The money Curtis used to finance me, and "Hazel," became a *creative instrument*. A creator *unpublished*, or *unseen,* is not a creator at all. Conversely, a magazine without creators is not a magazine. But the two together, working for and sharing the same interests, can make beautiful music together.

When capital respects creativity, you may well find them hand in hand, laughing all the way to the bank.

In this kind of relationship, in this joint exchange, who is the true creator? Both are natural allies who complement each other. Both earn and deserve, not disdain, each other's mutual respect and cooperation.

Creative people, it seems to me, have the will and the ability to make wondrous things happen that have never happened before—for the good of the creative man himself and for the good of all men. Creative people wish to add, not subtract from the world, and the world is better for this wish. Who are these people, these creators? I know them as my fellow artists. You, as your friends in the world of finance.

The reaction to the words of Ted Key was more than I dared hope for; it was quite unnecessary for me to say anything else. For in addition to Ted Key, at my side was the beloved Hazel, and who would argue with Hazel?

First impressions or last impressions notwithstanding, it is content and delivery that will mark the individual as a great or outstanding speaker. Content and delivery are the inevitable result of adequate research and preparation. When the speaker knows that the content of his speech is excellent, his delivery will be aided by his confidence and well-being, which are infectious. During the research phase these questions should be asked and should be readily answerable by the program chairman:

1. Is the meeting a special event rather than part of a continuing series of meetings?
2. If part of a continuing series, is the audience mainly the same each year?
3. Are copies of previous speeches available?
4. Who will precede and who will follow?
5. Will the speech be recorded or transcribed for reprinting?
6. Will there be attendance by the press?
7. Mixed audience, or any clergy present?
8. What facilities available for visual or audio supplements?
9. What is the desired length of the speech and will questions be invited?

10. What is Charter of Organization or objectives?

One rule-of-thumb for me has been four hours of preparation to one hour of speaking. My preparation has included trying out parts of the speech in conversations with various friends and associates. I found I was the least effective with newly written, not previously articulated material.

Years of practice have made it possible for me to appear to be giving an extemporaneous speech when, in fact, the speech has been written, parts of it rehearsed several times, and largely memorized. At one point I made myself independent of even written notes or outlines by having key words written on my fingers and palms of my hands!

I found it possible to be more emotional in a speech before a large audience than I would have dared be in a one-to-one conversation or with a small group. The risk of emotionalism can be eliminated by attribution of heavily charged statements to well-known people. In other words, if there is a sentiment that fits, it is often possible to find a quotation of a great man or woman who said it—and probably better than you could! "A coward dies a thousand deaths; a brave man dies but once," speaks beautifully about courage. Frankly, I would be embarrassed to make a similar statement on my own, but I would have no reluctance about using those quoted lines. My speech file is now bulging with quotations I have gathered over the years. *The New York Times* now has a "Quotation of the Day" insert, for instance, and once in a while there is one worth clipping. There is generally some phrase in every worthwhile book which could be useful sometime.

For this chapter, I reummaged through my speech file and selected various quotes that I have used with good effect before a wide variety of audiences. Some may be useful as is, others may stimulate thought or research for your speech file, should you decide to develop one.

After a particularly long and too-flattering introduction—which I anticipated—I quoted Emerson in my opening line: "Every hero becomes a bore at last." At an advertiser meeting in Los Angeles I got a fine reaction to the comment of Director

Joseph von Sternberg about Hollywood: "You can seduce a man's wife here, attack his daughter and wipe your hands on his canary bird, but if you don't like his movie, you're dead." When introduced as the author of four books (with the expectation of four more) I quoted Voltaire, who wrote bleakly about authors: "The only reward is contempt if one fails and hatred if one succeeds."

If you are ever introduced as "an expert" and sense any resentment from the audience, you can give your description of an expert as "anybody thirty miles from home."

A very dear friend who knew he would be introduced as "an egghead" used Louis Bromfield's marvelous description of one:

A person of spurious intellectual pretensions, often a professor or the protégé of a professor. Fundamentally superficial, over-emotional, and feminine in reactions to any problem. Supercil-ious and surfeited with conceit and contempt for the experience of more sound and able men. Essentially confused in thought and immersed in a mixture of sentimentality and violent evangelism. A doctrinaire supporter of Middle-European socialism as opposed to Greco-French-American ideas of democracy and liberalism. Subject to the old-fashioned philosophical morality of Nietzsche which frequently leads him into jail or disgrace. A self-conscious prig, so given to examining all sides of a question that he becomes thoroughly addled while remaining always in the same spot. An anemic bleeding heart.

He won over the audience, not by refuting it but by delivering a speech which showed he was everything the egghead in the description was not.

I was hard pressed for an opening line when invited to ad-dress a group participating in a benefit performance of a new Broadway play that had success written all over it. We were to go from an early buffet dinner to the opening night. The group was well lubricated so I used the very cutting description of firstnight audiences by Marc Klaw, theater critic and reviewer. He said they were "habitués and sons-of-habitués." That so-bered the group up.

If you are ever faced by an audience of critics, you can use these words of Jean Léon Gérôme, the nineteenth-century French painter and sculptor, to demonstrate the idiocy of some critics, "We are living in a century of decline and imbecility. The legacy contains pictures by Monet and Pissarro, doesn't it? For the state to accept such filth can only indicate moral blight. Anarchists and madmen."

In a political context, the tongue-in-cheek advice of Nathaniel Ward could be a good opener:

> For he that writes in such an age,
> When parties do for power enrage
> Ought to choose one side for right
> And then with all his wit and spite
> Blacken and vex the opposite.
> Scurrility's a useful trick
> Approved by the most politic,
> Fling dirt enough, and some will stick.

As the well-known target of a slander attack, I got appreciation from an audience with this advice to slanderers: Cut men's throats with whisperings. (Victorian saying)

Some one liners I often find useful, by Aneurin Bevin, that late head of Great Britain's Labour Party, are:

> Capitalism proudly displays medals won in the battles it has lost.

> There is no immaculate conception of disaster.

> Oh, the brave music of the *distant* drum.

> The establishment? I mean those people who have arrived and don't wish to depart.

Where does public speaking fit in the effective armament of the Billion Dollar Persuader? I would put it second on the list after credibility. I know that in my case my ability to speak well and effectively gave me an enormous advantage over my associates, some of whom were at least my equal in education, intelligency, and energy. I believe I would have reached the upper middle level of management without that characteristic. But having it was the difference between that level and positions as president and chairman of the board.

BDP Commandment 45 • **Is the potential gain equivalent to the energy required in the research, preparation, and delivery of a speech? If not, decline.**

BDP Commandment 46 • **Assemble all critical information about the audience, size, composition, age, education, and economic levels.**

BDP Commandment 47 • **Establish the philosophical thrust of your speech before a word is written.**

BDP Commandment 48 • **Write an outline of the speech; consider embellishments if necessary or desired—slides, charts or graphs, recordings, or videotapes, films, etc.**

BDP Commandment 49 • **Plan an amiable response to the introduction of the Master of Ceremonies. If necessary, give the MC something you can respond to with grace and humor.**

BDP Commandment 50 • **Unless a somber event, get your audience laughing as soon as possible by a story keyed to the event. For**

example, Mayor Jimmy Walker of New York made the principal address at a Washington's Birthday Celebration. He said Washington was "first in war, first in peace, first in the hearts of his countrymen...but he married a widow."

BDP Commandment 51 • Learn to wait for audience response to humor or emotional appeals. "The pregnant pause" is a most useful device for the effective speaker.

★★★

11

Using All the Clubs
★★★★★★★★★★★★★★★★★★★★★★★★★★★★★

Golf has always been considered the ideal
businessman's game. During the course of one round of golf at
the Blind Brook Club in Westchester, I overheard one of the
foursome say casually to John Griswold, "Does Grace [W.R.
Grace] have any interest in the oil business?" John Griswold,
one of the executive vice presidents of W.R. Grace asked,
"What is the ticket?" meaning, how much money would be
involved. The other man said, "About five million." That was
the entire conversation about oil during that golf round.

Three weeks later I read that W.R. Grace had joined a consortium to explore for oil in Libya. A year later the word was
released that the largest producing well in that part of the world
had been hit.

Quite apart from the advantage golf provides in putting customers and persuaders together for up to five hours, is what it
does *for* the golfer, himself. Golf is a lesson in life. It was never
put better than by the late Ellis Knowles, the greatest amateur
golfer in the United States for the longest period of time. I deeply
respected this charming, rugged, and courageous man. During

my earlier days at golf I played with Ellis as often as possible, learning something new in every round. One day, when I was playing miserably, unable to concentrate because of other problems, he calmly said, "You know, Joe, what makes golf the greatest game? You must learn to beat yourself before you can beat a golf course." I got the message, calmed down, and "shot the lights out," as the saying goes.

Golf encourages overview, for golf is an interrelationship of earth, water, wind, human beings, and mechanical devices. There are fourteen clubs in the completely equipped golf bag. One, the driver, can hit a ball well over three hundred yards, at the cost of one stroke. The other clubs hit the ball for lesser distances, at various elevations, and the putter, which at times hits the ball just a few inches, also at the cost of one stroke. During a round of golf, on a very good golf course, a golfer may actually use every club in the bag at least once. Is one club more important than another? Not really, in the overview. A driver would be useless in a sand trap, and a wedge (which is built to give loft to a shot) would be useless if the golfer has to hit a ball a longish distance under some tree limbs.

In persuasion there are many, many techniques and devices that can be used with astounding effectiveness, if the persuader is creative and original. These come easily to mind.

Telegrams

When I was in charge of the marketing of *The Today Show,* I made the policy decision that one of our primary targets for advertising would be the automotive field. The reason was simplicity itself. Within minutes after viewing "Today" millions of people would get into their cars to drive either to jobs or rairoad stations. And millions of people would drive to schools and shopping centers. We explained these obvious facts to the automobile manufacturers and their advertising agencies, and gained some very good schedules. We scored a major coup during announcement time by getting the New York City police to cordon off 49th Street during certain hours of the morning, so that the new models could be driven up to the window of the "Today" studio, and parked there while Dave Garroway strolled out of the studio and walked around the cars, pointing out their virtues. When we had all the schedules we could handle from the automobile manufacturers, we went after what we called "the aftermarket." This was the parts and service business—a multimillion-dollar industry with some very substantial advertisers with good budgets. During those days I considered it a personal affront to make an advertising presentation and not get an order. Our New England sales manager asked me to make a call on a company named Fram, which made automobile oil filters. The head of Fram was a delightful gentleman named Steve Wilson. His business was very good. I knew that because he maintained a beautiful home in New England, a home in Miami, and owned and raced horses. My first meeting with Steve Wilson was a disaster. He was very cordial when the meeting opened, but when he heard the proposal that Fram advertise between 7:00 and 9:00 in the *morning* he looked at me with complete disbelief. To him, the idea that anyone would turn on a television set at that time of the morning was insane.

I retreated and tried to figure out some way of shocking Steve Wilson, who dismissed rating reports and all other evidences that people did, indeed, tune in in the early morning. An idea surfaced, but it was dangerous. My thought was to get the names of two hundred Fram dealers around the United States, send them telegrams asking them to wire, collect, the answers to the following questions. Do you know who Dave Garroway is? Do you watch the NBC "Today" TV program? If so, do you like the NBC "Today" TV program?

The risk was that no one would send us a telegram, even though NBC would pay for it. Should that happen and word get out, even among our own people, it would be bad for their morale. Also, there was turnover, and I could imagine the high glee at ABC and CBS if a former employee of "Today" spread the word that "Culligan struck out." So, without telling anybody but my most trusted associate, we sent out two hundred telegrams to Fram dealers and waited. There was a trickle during the first three days, then a dozen wires arrived, then a score of wires came in, all saying just what we hoped. Yes, they knew who Dave Garroway was. Yes, they did watch "The Today Show" and they liked it.

I assembled the wires, asked for another appointment with Steve Wilson, and had one of the more delightful experiences of my life at NBC. Having a very good memory I was able to say to Steve Wilson, "Steve, do you think Pat Kelly, or John Shane, or Bob Miller (etc., etc., etc.) ever watch 'The Today Show' on NBC-TV between seven and nine?" He scoffed. I opened my brief case and took out the more than a hundred wires, all bearing the names of Fram dealers, all stating that they watched and enjoyed the show, and were Dave Garroway fans. Steve Wilson fingered the wires, read and reread the names of *his* dealers, and said, "Goddamn, I wouldn't have believed it possible." We had a schedule from Fram that became a fixture on the "Today" client list. During the fifteen years Fram advertised, that corporation spent nearly two million dollars. My expenditure on the wires and travel to New England was less than a thousand dollars.

Letters

Sherwood Dodge was one of the most intelligent, thoughtful and experienced research men in the advertising business in New York. He died far too young, unfortunately. I think of him often, because of the letter campaign I waged against him at one stage of my career in magazines. I did not have the best story to tell in terms of statistics, but there were abstract values I had to upgrade in his mind to justify the higher cost per thousand readers of my magazine. I decided on a series of one- and two-line notes to Sherwood Dodge, getting across one slender point at a time. The notes could be serious or funny, sophisticated or corny. After six months my salesman handling the agency started reporting new business for our magazine from that source. I adopted the technique with other prospects and continued it for several years. Long after abandoning the letters I had occasion to visit Sherwood Dodge in his office on an entirely different matter. He said, "Joe, I want to show you something." He went to his file, and took out a manila folder.

He handed it to me. It contained all thirty-two notes I had sent him years before. He said, "That was the best media promotion I can remember. I got to look forward to your notes. The irregular arrival was brilliant. The accumulated effect got you the business."

Hand Props

In one multimillion-dollar sale, all but one of the buying group was completely sold. The holdout was a notorious discount seeker. Before the critical meeting I visited a novelty store and acquired a large, bogus hypodermic syringe. As the meeting progressed to the critical point, and the holdout nagged about a reduced price, I took off my jacket, rolled up my sleeve and appeared to drive the needle into the vein. My associate pulled back the plunger and the large glass vial appeared to be filled with my blood. I said, "My God, Pete, what do you want ...blood?" We got the order—unanimously.

Adequate Research

When I headed the NBC Radio Network, our Chicago office needed the business of the Admiral Corporation. Admiral, brilliantly led by Ross Siragusa, had been in bitter competition with the giants in home appliances: General Electric, Westinghouse, and the Radio Corporation of America (RCA). But Siragusa had outthought and outpromoted the best minds in the industry.

The NBC people in Chicago were desperate and finally concluded that only I could crack Siragusa. That should have been enough to keep me away, but I wanted to meet Siragusa because he was known as one of the toughest negotiators in America.

The Chicago office sent me an intelligence report on Admiral's needs and objectives. Without checking the accuracy of that report, I designed a beautiful presentation which proudly boasted of NBC's ability to solve the problem. Perfect, eh? Put yourself in the buyer's shoes, right?

The big day came. I was ushered into the office of Ross Siragusa, accompanied by the regional sales manager and the head of sales for NBC in Chicago, who insisted on carrying the presentation into the office. One of them intoned pompously, "And *this,* Mr. Siragusa, is Matthew J. Culligan, *President* of the NBC Radio Network." All he needed was a fanfare.

Siragusa, a handsome, dapper man, rose from his chair, came around his huge desk, and, before our astonished group, knelt down and bowed with his head touching the floor. That was as close to fainting as I think I've ever come. He brought us back to near normalcy by extending his hand for a strong handshake and flashing a warm grin. The sales manager hurriedly got out of harm's way after his disastrous introduction and the floor was mine.

The presentation was good and dramatic. By an arrangement of sliding panels, I was able to bring out wings on both sides, top and bottom, so that the final mass nearly filled the end of his office. I concluded with the request for the order, "Since," I added, "this program was specifically designed for the problems of Admiral."

Siragusa looked at the massive display, at me, at the conclusions and recommendations, and back to me. Then he rose and said, "Mr. Culligan, that is a brilliant solution to an Admiral problem—which we solved *four months ago.*"

That was it. Weeks of work, over a thousand dollars in cost, and we were stone cold dead.

In Ross Siragusa's case, I returned with another presentation, this time for Curtis, some four years later. This time I went alone, sat modestly at his desk, and outlined my program. He bought a $2.5 million advertising-merchandising package. We became and remained good friends, a symbol of which was his insistence that I use his forty-two-foot fishing boat when I was in Palm Beach.

Always probe further than the information you have at hand to make sure that a prospect's situation hasn't changed.

Promotion Tools

The "Monitor" radio show was a critical success, but slow in attracting advertisers. Its critical promotion period was the summer, when millions left their television sets and turned to radio, often in their car as they traveled or while they were at poolside or the beach. Our group brainstormed and decided on a promotion gimmick which, even fifteen years later, is still remembered and revered. All the principal buyers received an enormous bath towel on which was printed, "Dry up—and listen to *Monitor!*"

Alertness

Necessity is truly the mother of invention in persuasion. At one point in my business life I was advertising director of *Modern Bride Magazine*. It was a bad second in a two-book field, the bridal field being completely dominated by *Bride's Magazine*. There was no hope of overtaking *Bride's Magazine* in editorial excellence or circulation, so in desperation—the head of the company said make it profitable or liquidate it—I devised a merchandising scheme with the great buying office for department stores, AMC. I persuaded AMC's Irene Bender to get a group of manufacturers together for a chainwide bridal promotion, with the agreement that the stores would handle the merchandise they advertised in *Modern Bride*. The stores agreed to give windows and instore displays to the advertised products. When the manufacturers had been told by AMC, I then called with my salesmen to get them to agree to run full page ads at their expense. When the magazine was mentioned, often derisively, I said, "Look, even if we forgot to print your ad, the program will succeed because of the merchandising. Get aboard!" *Modern Bride* ran a twenty-four-page section in one issue, the biggest such insert up to that time. From that point on, the magazine improved its editorial content, and out-merchandised *Bride's Magazine*, ultimately becoming the most successful book in the bridal field. The bridal field was expanded by the success of *Modern Bride*. We forced *Bride's Magazine* to improve. They now run neck and neck.

Gimmicks

After "The Today Show" succeeded on NBC, our group, Dick Pinkham, Mort Werner and I, gained some celebrity within NBC. We were given the great opportunity to launch "The

Tonight Show" with Steve Allen. Repeating promotions was anathema to me, so I thought long and hard about a gimmick for "The Tonight Show" with its great cast. In addition to Steve Allen the show featured Edie Gorme, Steve Lawrence, and Andy Williams, all new talent to network television. While making a call on Madison Avenue I was almost run down by a coffee wagon enroute to one of the buildings that housed many advertising agencies. An idea popped out of my subconscious. I rushed back to NBC and directed the promotion department to make a deal with the company that owned the coffee carts to overprint, on all cups and napkins, the words THE TONIGHT SHOW WITH STEVE ALLEN, PREMIERING TONIGHT!!! We blanketed the entire advertising community during the day of the initial broadcasting of "The Tonight Show." Unlike "Today," which got off to a painfully slow and expensive start, "The Tonight Show" with Steve Allen was an immediate hit. Steve Allen was followed by Jack Paar, and then Johnny Carson for whom the show seemed to have been specially crafted. "Tonight," in its third decade, has grossed scores of millions for NBC.

Emotional Appeals

There are circumstances in which emotional appeals are justified. If the cause is worthwhile and the motivation is high, an appeal to the emotions can offset statistical deficiencies. When *The Saturday Evening Post* was near extinction because of mismanagement of the Curtis Publishing Company, I made what was, very frankly, an appeal to the emotions of the men who were running America's leading corporations, knowing that most of them were raised in families in which *The Saturday Evening Post* was a fixture, to be read by every adult and child in the family. And many of the top executives of America actually were small town delivery boys, delivering the *Post*, *Country Gentleman*, and other Curtis magazines, for "points" with which they could get sports equipment and bicycles. I recall saying, "We can't let this great American institution die." When it became apparent that the *Post* would weather the storm, I hired a top advertising agency executive, Bud MacNelly, as the first publisher of *The Saturday Evening Post*. He was a brilliant speaker, and he caught the spirit of the *Post* immediately. He could make emotional appeals at will, and literally bring tears to the eyes of his more impressionable prospects reminding them how they sat at their fathers's knees and learned about *The Saturday Evening Post*. Emotionalism can backfire, so use it with great care.

Humor

Laughter, chuckles, and smiles relieve tension, reduce stress, and open the mind. Any meeting that opens with a good, well-told story has a better chance of being successful. One meeting I attended in Baton Rouge started out badly because of the clumsiness of the MC. The principal speaker was a psychiatrist, who was appealing for industry support for a new mental hospital. The men and women in the audience were the principal executives of all the important corporations in that part of Louisiana. The doctor knew the atmosphere was strained. He rose and in one sentence completely reversed the ambiance. He said, "Ladies and gentlemen, as a psychiatrist I have a great sense of comfort looking at this large, affluent audience of business leaders, knowing full well that in time a good percentage of you will be patients of mine." The audience exploded with appreciative laughter, and he had them in the palm of his hand for the remainder of the speech.

Several very key factors should be remembered. If just one person in an audience is offended by an off-color story, it should not have been told. Even a good, funny story can be ineffective if it is entirely pointless for the meeting. And it should always be possible for a speaker to find a story with pertinence to his audience.

Attention-getting tricks do not have to be verbal or involved. One trick I employed was to say, elaborately, "Ladies and gentlemen, we must always remember *three* things," and hold up *two* fingers. A few would get it immediately, then the rest would catch on. Not good for a guffaw, but always a chuckle.

An old friend, now dead, opened his speech by having a dozen ushers deliver a wrapped book, which he would describe as his newest creation and a gift to all his listeners. He would then ask to open the package and remove the book, the title of which was *What I Have Learned in Twenty Five Years in Publishing.* The audience discovered that the book was two hundred blank pages!

The memories keep flooding back, and I have been feeling real joy as I have written about these true experiences. I could overdo it, so I will now make the simple point that human imagination and alertness and sensitivity are sometimes more important to the persuader than dollars. It is my fond hope that, if you are in business, you will be stimulated by these stories to look for unique and original ways to attract attention to your products and services, and register their selling points with wit and intelligence and humor. The same applies if you are in public service, education, or politics.

BDP Commandment 52 • **Do not let your thinking be restricted to the usual, routine practices.**

BDP Commandment 53 • **Tension and stress are blocks to good interpersonal relationships. They can be melted by good humor, friendliness, and concern.**

BDP Commandment 54 • **If the persons you are trying to persuade see many other competitors during the day or week, think out how you can stand out in first and last impressions.**

BDP Commandment 55 • Do not tell an off-color story if there is a possibility that one person in the audience will be offended.

12

Evil Persuasion
★★★★★★★★★★★★★★★★★★★★★★★★★★★★

In a business career extending over almost four decades I have been amazed by how very few evil people I have met. Not looking for them might have had something to do with that, but I was raised in a family that had its philosophy set by my mother. Time after time, when anyone was being criticized in my mother's presence, she would say, "We're all God's children," and that would generally end the matter. If it didn't my mother would simply walk away.

It is sometimes difficult to accept my mother's philosophy when I consider those types whom I consider truly evil: doctors who violate their oaths; lawyers who operate from a privileged sanctuary and cheat defenseless old people and dependent young people; lawyers who are known as "undertakers" and who are expert in burying reputations; news reporters and editors who lie; libelers and slanderers; poison-pen-letter writers; bearers of false witness; unprincipled prosecuting attorneys; corrupters of young, innocent boys and girls; child molesters and abusers of children.

You might wonder why I would include newspaper reporters

and editors among the truly evil. It is because they are violating a trust. The law has protected them to an extraordinary degree, almost always supporting the strictest construction of the First Amendment: "Congress shall pass no law abridging the freedom of speech, and of the press." The sole exception has been when the First Amendment conflicts with the Sixth Amendment—the right to a public trial by an impartial jury.

During the late 1960s I was the recipient of the Silver Anvil Award of the Public Relations Society of America for my improvement of the image of the Curtis Publishing Company in the financial circles of business and industry. When I took over the company in June of 1962 it was, by concensus, ninety days from bankruptcy. I achieved three massive new refinancing programs, one for $22 million, one for $26 million and the third, for $38 million, startlingly material facts in the revitalization of Curtis.

But at the critical point in the negotiations for the $38 million loan, several editors of *The Saturday Evening Post* ran a story that accused two national sports figures of a college football fix. These two sports notables sued Curtis for $10 million each. Within a month a half-dozen other men and women who had also been subjects of *Post* articles filed suits for an additional $18 million. Little wonder that the MC, in his introduction, called me "one of America's greatest part-time libel experts." There was appreciative laughter in which I did not share. The sloppy research and writing and editing of the story in the *Post* cost the Curtis Publishing Company over one million dollars in settlements and lawyers fees. I should have fired those who were responsible for that disaster. I did not. That error was to cost me dearly.

Persuading the bankers to whom we had presented the new refinancing plan to ignore the libel suits threatening Curtis was a personal feat of which I was very proud. Little did I dream that I, within two years, would be the target for libel plus slander by the very same editors who had libeled the sports figures.

Libel and slander are forms of attempted persuasion the objective of which is the denigration or destruction of the victims. Slander and libel are usually joined in the minds of most people. There is a dread difference between the two. Libel is analogous to armed robbery, slander to being slowly poisoned.

The victim of libel knows his attacker and "sees" the weapon, for libel must be both written and published, not in the sense that a newspaper is published, of course, but *distributed* to others. For example, if I wrote you, the reader, a letter accusing you of terrible crimes it would *not* constitute libel. But sending copies of that letter to others could constitute libel.

The victim of slander has no such advantages. Slander is accomplished entirely by spoken words and gestures. The victim may not know about the slanders for some time—weeks, months, even years. Because of the lamentable appetite of many people for gossip, the "slow poison" may circulate very widely. The sources of the slander may be obscured completely as the spoken charges are repeated and often embellished. Few slanders can be traced to the source. Fortunately very few readers of this book will ever have the problems I faced in the wake of a corporate take-over attempt. But if any reader does, I exhort him to look in the mirror and see to what degree he might have been responsible for his vulnerability. When I did, it became apparent that my lack of experience in corporate warfare made me vulnerable.

The decision I made to take my beating with as much style and grace as possible was not overlooked by the press and the heads of various businesses and members of boards of directors. I was immediately offered the presidency of Burns International Security Services for which I wrote a complete plan for the Servo-Electro-Mechanical Industrial Security, a concept that changed the industry. The lure of communications was too strong, so I accepted the presidency of the Mutual Broadcasting Company, the world's largest radio network. With a new cadre I was able to put it into a strong profit position and sold my stock (which I had bought for one dollar a share) for eighteen dollars a share. With some of the proceeds I acquired a part of the Teletape Corporation and was elected president of that production company, the biggest in videotape on the East Coast. It provided all the facilities for "Sesame Street" and "The Electric Company." It had severe problems relating to unions. They were resolved by the merger of Teletape with Reeves Studios, a process I started with a great persuader Hazard Reeves. His particular specialty was starting small companies and launching them on the American Stock Exchange.

It was then that I decided to leave the business world and establish a new base of credibility as a published author. There is a tyranny of literature in America that gives authors much more credit for assumed virtues than they deserve. In fact, writing a book or two may be the quickest way to national celebrity. *How to be a Billion Dollar Persuader* is my fourth book. My fifth, sixth, and seventh are in various stages of development. When I have established a new base of credibility it is my intention to use what powers of persuasion I have on behalf of the indigent old, the sick and the dependent young. Will you join me?

BDP Commandment 56 • **Do not do anything you would not want your worst enemy to find out about. He probably will.**

BDP Commandment 57 • **Next to control of the money (the real control of any situation), the control of promotions and raises is critical. Do not give this authority lightly.**

BDP Commandment 58 • **Beware of lawyers generally and particularly those who have been "undertakers" in past situations. Lawyers obey those who pay the bills.**

BDP Commandment 59 • **Do not ever trust a reporter unless he or she is your**

brother or sister, father or mother.

BDP Commandment 60 • There are situations that are so difficult to resolve that the solutions may become timebombs ticking away waiting to be ignited.

BDP Commandment 61 • There is no lasting gratitude for a manager from those he has saved from disaster.

BDP Commandment 62 • The press will always make headlines out of charges and often ignore vindication.

BDP Commandment 63 • Most bankers are gutless but a good and loyal one can truly be your best friend in business.

BDP Commandment 64 • During your early and middle years in business you never lose if you learn. Bad experiences are good teachers, too.

BDP Commandment 65 • Win, lose, or draw, do it with style and grace.

★★★

Epilogue

★★★★★★★★★★★★★★★★★★★★★★★★★★★★

Four events, so different they might have happened on different planets caused me to request from my publisher a delay in publication to give me time to write this epilogue. I felt the necessity to close this book on a more serious, and if possible, profound note.

During the fall of 1978 and the spring of 1979 the following occurred. The Reverend James Jones led over seven hundred adults to suicide and caused the parents among them to murder over two hundred and fifty children. The United States showed signs of political maturity in some of its major international relationships. A Polish cardinal became the first non-Italian Pope of the Roman Catholic Church in over four hundred years. The leaders of the People's Republic of China decided to seek normalized relationships with the United States after decades of isolation and hostility. Islamic Asia exploded joining Islamic Arabia in a towering new world force. What are the results?

Jim Jones will live in infamy as the most evil persuader of the closing decades of the twentieth century. Pope John Paul II may

159 •

build the bridge between the religious world and atheistic Communism. He may make the Catholic Church mean something again to present young and future generations. A billion Chinese with enormous oil resources can change the course of human events and cause the Soviet Union to behave in a less hostile and disruptive manner. The Soviet Union has more to fear from the Nation of Islam, meaning all the Muslims of the Asiatic and Arab worlds, than does the United States. The majority of Soviet citizens along the southern borders of the U.S.S.R. are Muslims. The potential power of their aroused spirituality is incalculable.

The closing decades of the twentieth century may be marked by more change than any period in human history. The opportunities for high level persuasion for both good and mischief will be heightened.

The fifteenth anniversary of the assassination of John Fitzgerald Kennedy came and went and I suddenly knew how this book should end. One could not think of his death without remembering also the cruel deaths of Robert Francis Kennedy and Martin Luther King, Jr.

Martin Luther King Jr. could have been the most destructive persuader in his time in the United States. If, during and after the race riots in Watts and Detroit and other cities when blacks shouted that they had had enough, the country could have plunged into a bloody civil war, black against white, if Martin Luther King had elected to go that terrible route. But that great man could not abandon his lifelong beliefs about the poor, the disadvantaged, the sick, the indigent and the dependent young. So he worked to heal the wounds of the country.

The remembrance of the deaths of these three compassionate men sent me to my files for some lines of poetry that literally brought tears to my eyes not long after President Kennedy's assassination.

> And when he fell in whirlwind, he went down
> As when a lordly cedar, green with boughs,

Goes down with a great shout upon the hills,
And leaves a lonesome place against the sky.

Charles Edwin Markham wrote that about an earlier Billion Dollar Persuader, Abraham Lincoln. It applies equally to John F. Kennedy, Martin Luther King, Jr. and Robert Kennedy. This is not the digression it may seem to be, for there is a point to be made about the power of words. There is still "a lonesome place against the sky," for the Kennedys and King were persuaders of a somewhat different kind. They were persuaders on behalf of the poor, the weak, the young, and the disadvantaged. Our country desperately needs someone to fill that lonesome place against the sky who has the ability to persuade millions of Americans that we are committing a kind of soul suicide by not taking proper care of our indigent old, the sick, and the dependent young in our country, the most prosperous large country in the world. It is my fondest hope that some young readers of this book may decide to become Billion Dollar Persuaders on behalf of those who cannot help themselves. If you are a natural born persuader then perhaps you should give something back to the beneficient nature (or God) from whom you received that priceless gift. If you have been made a persuader by life experiences and training you can avoid that "awfulness" that Yves St. Laurent complained about by involving yourself in good causes. There is no better cause than aiding the old, the indigent, the sick and the dependent young. Use your powers of persuasion on their behalf and you will not be committing the soul suicide of past generations who have left you the present problems to clean up. Farewell and good persuading.